Write Ways to WIN WRITING CONTESTS

How to Join the Winners' Circle for Prose and Poetry Awards

ABOUT THE AUTHOR

John Howard Reid has worked in the publishing industry all his life. Starting as a humble subscription agent, he rose from the ranks to own and manage book and magazine publishers, retail bookstores, wholesale book distributors and wholesale newsagents. In 1985, he began to publish his own novels under the "Merryll Manning" pseudonym. Over the years, these seventeen books received enormous critical acclaim and were reprinted in various editions by other publishers including Harper/Collins. In 2009, these novels, commencing with *Merryll Manning: Trapped on Mystery Island* and *Merryll Manning: The Health Farm Murders*, have finally made their USA debut. Under his own name, John Howard Reid has also published thirty books of movie history/film criticism in the "Hollywood Classics" series.

In order to research *Write Ways To Win Writing Contests*, John Howard Reid wrote a number of short prose pieces and poems, which he entered in eighty writing contests over an eighteen-month period, winning a string of prizes and awards, including First Prize for Non-Fiction in the prestigious Southern Cross Literary Competition 2002; First Prize in the Play/Screenplay section in the Gold Coast Literary Awards 2003; the Hills Library Prize for Prose 2002; Central Coast Writers' Festival, Second Prize 2003; Sun City Poetry Awards, Third Prize 2003; plus a large number of Very Highly Commended, Highly Commended and Commended certificates.

For the past seventeen years, John Howard Reid has served as chief judge for the Tom Howard Short Story, Essay and Prose Contest, one of the world's top literary competitions. He also judges the annual Tom Howard Poetry Contest, as well as the Margaret Reid Prize for Traditional Verse.

Write Ways to WIN WRITING CONTESTS

How to Join the Winners' Circle for Prose and Poetry Awards

NEW EXPANDED EDITION

by

John Howard Reid

LULU BOOKS
2009

Revised Third Edition: Published March, 2004

Completely Revised Fourth Edition: March, 2009

http://writeway.exactpages.com

ISBN: 978-0-557-02325-7

INTRODUCTION

Creditable Credits

If you're seeking technical advice on how to write effective English, how to put the proper word in its proper place, you've come to the wrong book. On the other hand, if you feel you have mastered enough elementary techniques and now wish to step out of the amateur class and learn how to become a <u>successful</u> writer, this little handbook is for you.

For the actual art, craft and technique of writing, a multitudinous array of instructive how-to-write guides are readily available. The budding author can soon learn all about grammar, punctuation, and even more importantly, style. One vital area that is often not represented, however, is a book of sound advice on mastering the first rung on the ladder of success, namely preparing and submitting manuscripts to literary competitions.

In his Preface to the 2003 Gold Coast Anthology of Winning Stories, Poems and Plays, John O'Reilly writes: "I would encourage all entrants to continue with their writing, to keep entering writing competitions... Many successful authors started by entering competitions, thus making the first step towards achieving their goal."

I believe all of us have at least three or four really great stories locked in our hearts. I also believe all of us can learn how to transmit these stories to paper and make them come alive. Unfortunately, there are very few books that tell us what to do once we've got the finished manuscripts in our hands.

I want to be a writer. I want to be a good writer. That's an admirable ambition, and it's one that almost everyone can achieve. Some of us may have more natural gifts, but every budding author can learn effective ways to apply the techniques of our craft. Once we've reached this stage, however, what we really need to know, what we <u>must</u> know if we are to proceed further, is how we become <u>successful</u> writers.

All of us have our own agendas. All of us want to do our own thing. All of us have a desire to share what we believe is our own unique vision. But that direct appeal is not always the way to achieve success. Not always and not usually. Of course, there are always exceptions. However, as a general rule, we must approach our goal obliquely. Not directly. That's why we enter literary contests and competitions. To amass credits. To achieve publication. To build and build on our initial successes until finally we achieve the sort of independence that enables us to write effectively on the subjects we most care about.

CHAPTER ONE

Know Your Contest

If you just want to do your own thing and are not really serious about <u>winning</u>, this is not the handbook for you. On the other hand, if you really want to take that first giant step as an author and achieve such recognition and success that <u>anything</u> you write will automatically climb at least halfway up the bestseller list, the first thing you must do is win a major literary prize.

True, there are other ways. Get yourself elected President or Prime Minister, for example; or marry a super-star; or take up professional baseball, golf, tennis or football. Or even just happen along to a desperate publisher at just the right moment with just the right substitute manuscript for the one Mr Desperate has just lost to a competitor.

For most of us, however, well-known creative writing awards are not only the best option, they're the only option!

Obstacles still abound, of course. Many well-publicized prizes like the Nobel, the Pulitzer and the Mann-Booker are only available to already published work. Most are also limited by other constraints. The Mann-Booker, for instance, is awarded only to British residents or British Commonwealth authors who are published in Great Britain. Publication elsewhere doesn't count!

Not all of us can win First Prize, of course. To research this book, I entered exactly eighty contests in eighteen months, but only achieved three First Prizes, one Second Prize, and one Third! Fortunately, two of those winning awards were handed out by prestigious contests, particularly the 2002 Southern Cross Literary Competition, judged by Judith Rodriguez, who is generally regarded as one of the top literary critics in the country.

Cash prizes certainly come in very handy. But while the money is nice, and major prizes are definitely most welcome, even more pleasing to me is the fact that I won a total of fourteen Very Highly Commended, Highly Commended and Commended awards. In addition, my entries were short-listed on at least five other occasions. (I say *at least five*, because most contests do NOT publish details of their short list).

Never underestimate these minor distinctions. They're all valuable. For many reasons. Firstly, they look great on a résumé. Secondly, they show that our cash-winning places were not just a fluke. They prove we're reliable, dedicated and highly skilled writers with something important to communicate. Like pure entertainment.

To me, entertainment ranks number one as a writer's objective. Never under-rate its importance. Never join the dismissive snobs who say, "Oh, he's only a Detective writer!" or "Oh, she's only a Romance author!" Would you believe even some of the world's greatest writers found themselves constantly subjected to this sort of criticism. The English humorist, P.G. Wodehouse (whose books sold in the millions in the 1920s and 1930s), was constantly put down by the literary establishment. He used to refer his scoffers to a passage in the Talmud where one of the Old Testament prophets met up with a couple of wandering minstrels. The prophet asked what they did for a living. They replied: "We travel around the country, singing songs, telling funny stories or spinning adventurous tales, trying to cheer people up!" The prophet commented: "How noble! How unselfish! What could be more praiseworthy than lifting people's troubles by bringing smiles to their lips and gladness to their hearts!"

Back to awards. Yes, it is nice to come first. Very rewarding emotionally and financially. But it is not something all of us can do all the time, or even most of the time. My aim is to accumulate credits to impress potential publishers and agents. An editor is more likely to have faith in my ability if he sees a page or two of solid credits on my résumé rather than just one or two highly regarded First Prizes. Everyone knows that an author can come out of left field, knock off one or even two winners, but then never come within a mile of repeating that performance for the rest of his or her life. Margaret Mitchell is a famous case, but there are plenty of others like Thomas Heggen (who wrote *Mr Roberts*). Writing a best-seller can be compared with winning a lottery. Just as many lucky-streak authors have emerged in literature as in any other human endeavor. Perhaps more! But I'd rather be recognized for my talent than simply my good fortune.

CHAPTER TWO

Awards? Prizes? Contests?

What's the difference between an Award and a Prize, a Contest and a Competition? Thirty years ago, Awards and Prizes were strictly limited only to published books and authors, whereas humble contests and competitions catered for original, unpublished manuscripts. In recent years, however, the distinction has become extremely blurred. For example, The Vance Palmer *Prize* for Fiction is offered only to *published* work, but the W.B. Yeats Poetry *Prize* is awarded strictly to *unpublished* typescripts. All four terms – award, prize, contest, competition – are now interchangeable.

In any event, most of us can't offer a published book. And even if we could, we wouldn't need to worry our little heads about submitting it for any relevant awards. That's something that publishers traditionally handle. And they do it well. Many a delighted author, surprised by the sudden onslaught of media attention, has exclaimed, "I didn't even know my book was entered!"

We'd certainly love to be in that position too, but thus far our only contact with publishers has probably been through a wall of rejection slips. We have accumulated stacks of manuscripts, stored in odd drawers or old suitcases around the house (or better still, on CDs or floppy disks). So we need to find a contest or a competition or an award or a prize that actively seeks unpublished work. It's a shame we're forced to bypass many of the better-publicized events, but there's still plenty of glitter from which to choose.

However, our next problem is length. Many contests impose limits that severely constrain creativity. If all our stories range above 5,000 words for example, or all our poems are longer than 50 lines, finding a suitable contest will often entail consulting a guide like The Open Directory.

But length is not our only concern. The prestige and standing of the contest are paramount. It's not much use winning a prize in a contest organized by the Lower Boondoggle Writers' Group whose membership consists of two or three keen but unrecognized fanatics.

So how do you separate the sheep from the goats? The prizes provide the key. If the cash awards seem ridiculously high, there is generally (though not always) a catch. And that catch is often (though again I stress, not always) the simple fact that either the prizes are not awarded at their full, advertised value, or they are offered on the basis of pure chance.

To deal with the last type of incident first, the pure-chance contest is actually not a "contest" at all. It's a lucky draw, in which winners are not selected on the basis of skill or creativity, but simply at random. True, the prizes are generally awarded, and you could be lucky. But prestige-wise, these "contests" count as dross.

Just as common and equally pernicious is the competition in which you will find (if you look really hard) a so-called "cancellation clause" or "pro-rata rule". The former will state (in extremely small print) that the organizers reserve the right to cancel the contest if a certain number of entries are not received. This number is often set at a ridiculously high figure. It's true, for instance, that a prestige poetry contest (like the Bridport Prize) will receive around five thousand entries. But five thousand people are not going to enter the Boondoggle Awards for Modern Verse. Not even five hundred! My guess would be closer to thirty. So if the Boondoggle Awards are set to be canceled if fewer than three hundred entries are received, give them a miss! And if you must enter the Boondoggle or somesuch, my rule is to never ever write a special piece for these contests. For instance, if Boondoggle wants poems or prose pieces on a particular subject, say *The Mystery of Levitation*, I'd never rise to the bait even if they offered five hundred dollars. There's a strong possibility the contest will be canceled, and an even stronger possibility that you won't collar the cash. So there you are, stuck with a well-researched entry on levitation that you can't use anywhere else. (Contest judges are a knowledgeable lot and they tend to look askance at any "open theme" submissions that were obviously intended for other events).

But that's not the end to Boondoggling. Just as infuriating is the "pro-rata rule". This allows the contest principals to lower the prize money in proportion to the number of entries received (or rather NOT received). It works like this: The advertised First Prize of $10,000 (in huge black-type lettering) will in fact only be paid if a minimum of two thousand entries (at ten dollars a time) are sent in. If only fifteen hundred are lodged, then the prizes will be reduced by a quarter. And so on.

Who oversees these contests, making sure that everything is on the up-and up? Answer: no-one.

So steer well clear of contests with cancellation and pro-rata provisions!

Publication of winning and selected entries in some sort of anthology by contest organizers, is another proviso that repels some writers. In this case, however, something needs to be said on the organizer's side.

Professional writers object to a competition that offers publication because once a story or poem is "published", it usually becomes ineligible for future contests. Most manuscript competitions stipulate that entries be "unpublished". On the other hand, organizers argue that the winning entries must be seen by all to be worthy of that honor. The *bona fides* of their competitions are at stake.

True, most critics would undoubtedly disagree with the final selections anyway, but no-one would argue that the contest was not properly judged by some person or persons qualified to act in that capacity. Someone with a university degree in English and/or a reasonably impressive body of creative work and/or some active connection with the publishing industry. (I qualify on all three scores). That doesn't prevent people questioning the judge's outlook, philosophy or convictions. But like him (or her) or not, the judge is the final arbiter. In almost all contests, the judge's awards are not only final, but his or her possibly quirky interpretations of the rules are likewise unchallengeable.

Usually, upcoming writers are more than happy to compete in "publication offered" contests. They haven't yet made a name for themselves. They feel it important to get their work before the public. And they're absolutely right!

I have struck some aspiring authors, however, who made it a practice to rarely or never enter literary contests. They had deluded themselves into thinking they would be competing with the likes of Tom Clancy or Kathleen Norris. This is far from the truth. As a general rule, best-selling and/or respectably established authors never enter creative writing competitions. For two main reasons: (1) No matter how high the prize, the amount is piddling compared to their normal earnings. (2) Almost all contests are judged anonymously. Imagine the chagrin of a famous writer who discovers that his opus barely rates a Commended certificate! The item would soon be picked up by the media and, in no time at all, your once-famous literary figure would become a laughing stock, the butt of late-night television comedians all over the country.

So what is the mark of a contest with prestige? Longevity is usually the number one yardstick. If a contest offers reasonably large prizes in return for comparatively modest entry fees (sometimes called "reading fees") and is now batting along with at least four or five previous annual events under its belt, you can be sure it has accumulated prestige. Particularly if the judges are reasonably well-known.

The next yardstick is to look closely at who is advertising the contest. This is far more important than who or what the actual organizing organization might be. Is the Contest listed on the web in the appropriate category (Writers' Resources: Contests/Short Stories, for example) in The Open Directory? Or in the writing contests category at Google or Yahoo. These engines (and others) are serviced by the Open Directory which abides by very strict rules. They don't just list any old contest that requests a listing. (Be careful that you don't confuse the clearly identified paid advertisements with the regular listing. Not that all paid advertising is suspect. Not by any means. But use the links provided to check them out).

The smart contestant will also check if the contest listing appears in highly reputable sites like Winning Writers and First Writer.

The organizers are the next and final key. Most contests are run by (in descending order of importance): (1) Writers' Associations, Groups, Sites and Societies; (2) Publishers (that's where I qualify. This is my forty-fifth year in book publishing); (3) Universities and other places of learning; (4) Trustees and executors for well-known benefactors; (5) Business corporations, councils, government departments, charities, professional associations, tourist destinations, etc., that on the face of it may have little to do with Literature, but sponsor a contest for publicity and prestige; (5) Private individuals.

All these categories, even the last, are usually highly trustworthy, although some society contests staffed by volunteers suffer from a poorly organized management. You can often add two or three months to the actual date when prizes are announced.

On the other hand, many authors are understandably wary of contests initiated by publishers where the sole prize is publication. Mind you, many extremely reputable, long-established firms use this tactic to stimulate submissions. The big advantage to the publisher is that his reading fees are then at least partly paid by the writer, thus very considerately reducing the publishers' overheads. Objecting writers, however, argue that publishers are filling their schedules on the cheap.

Personally, I don't mind forking out twenty or forty dollars to a household-name publisher for "reading fees". At least I can be sure the publisher is actually going to have the office boy glance at my manuscript in his lunch break, not merely direct him to re-route it to the slush pile.

As to which group is preferable, it's true that the literary establishment regards university sponsorship as the pinnacle of perfection. Why? For the simple reason that most university pundits and professors comprise the so-called "literary establishment".

On the other hand, I tend to avoid university and college contests, because what they seek is "Literature". I don't write Literature. I know it's wrong of me and highly insensitive, and I feel guilty as hell, but I'm not the slightest bit interested in hospitals, morgues, body fluids and exotic diseases, or even the plight of the Maori. (The only Maori I ever knew, a chap named Prosper Hoormai, had enough business acumen to sell his string of cinemas to some idiot corporation before television hit a home run and spent the rest of his life summering in his own mountain resort in sunny Saskatchewan and wintering in a splendid condominium he owned in Scottsdale, Arizona).

Both private individuals and corporations tend to be highly sensitive of their public image. They're my pick for reliability and trustworthiness.

Publishers, like literary societies, tend to be less reliable, mainly owing to the sheer volume of entries they receive.

Another problem with publishers is that a few self-styled "print publishers" who tend to push themselves to the forefront are actually not publishers at all but vanity presses. These I will deal with in a later chapter.

And then, of course, there are the internet contests. Most reputable contests will not accept internet submissions, because of the damage the internet does to formatting. True, there are some highly esteemed competitions that will accept entries both online and through the normal postal mail. Indeed, at the time I'm writing these words (early 2009), ALL the contests that accept entries by both postal and internet services are totally trustworthy.

However, a question mark lies with those competitions that insist entries be sent electronically only, either by direct email or by pasting in an online submission box. Most of these contests are not contests at all, but strictly lotteries.

CHAPTER THREE

Wrong Contests

These are simply contests that are wrong for you. In a later chapter, I'll talk about scam contests or risky contests.

In researching this book, I entered eighty competitions. Well, in point of fact, seventy-seven actually. Three were online competitions which don't really count, though I did well in them. The organizers of the Donard Prize (U.K.) gave me first place (among 673 contestants) in one of their short story awards, but I missed out on the popular vote. I entered two online Canadian poetry contests, achieving the short list at Mattia and coming in tenth at Tickled-by-Thunder.

Anyway, amongst the favored seventy-seven, I made the short list at least twenty-four times. That's almost a one-in-three success rate. However, I would have improved my score considerably if I had actually avoided contests in which I knew I stood little or no chance of success. But as I wanted to prove this very point (and also hopefully receive a parcel of judges' reports I could make use of), I entered them anyway.

The first thing, of course, is to appreciate your own limitations. I say *of course*, but you would be surprised how many successful artists long for acclaim in some other branch of their activities. The comedian longs for plaudits as a tragedian, the fashionable portraitist wonders why people are unwilling to snap up his landscapes, the master pianist would rather sing duets with Placido Domingo, while the crowd-pleasing mystery/suspense novelist has his eyes set on the Nobel Prize for Literature.

Sometimes, it's mighty hard to admit to ourselves that though we might be king pins as best-selling novelists, we

17

couldn't write a halfway decent poem for nuts.

Poetry is my weakness too. When it comes to the traditional sonnet or rhyming ballad, I'm absolutely hopeless. Mind you, I can write traditional verse, but only with a great deal of effort. The strain is very evident in the finished product.

So, although I might aspire to inherit the mantle of Carl Sandburg, it's really just a waste of time and money to enter a contest for traditional poetry. Free verse, fine! But anything calling for rhyme and meter, I'll leave to our current Wordsworths and Poes.

Similarly, I decline any calls for flash fiction (which is usually defined as short stories of less than 1,500 words). I like room to express myself. I'm not really comfortable in the short-short form. I've tried to write it, tried to like it, but it's just not me!

Knowing our limitations in genre, however, is merely the start. What about our temperament? Here, for example, is a contest that would suit us right down to the ground. Trouble is, we've just discovered the details. It closes in three weeks. And we don't have a suitable story on hand. We could dash one off, of course. But that's not the way we usually like to write. We like to revise and polish, give our words an immaculate sheen. In fact, that's the part we like best.

My advice, tempting though a contest might be, give it a miss if we don't have time to submit our very best.

Another problem arises when we are not quite happy with the rules. My advice—in fact, it's not advice, it's a command—don't, don't, don't submit!

You'd be amazed how many contestants try to get away with ignoring or breaking rules.

The most common crime relates to word limits. A category might call for 3,000 words but we've got this really great story that's only 863 words over. Who's going to notice?

I tell you right now that word limits are strictly enforced by almost all organizers. It's simply not fair to other contestants to allow anyone any leeway whatsoever. Good advice is to aim for at least twenty or thirty words under the limit, as some programs will include titles and subtitles, whilst others will not. Worst of all are hyphenated words which some count as a single, others as a double. (For this reason, it's a sensible idea NOT to justify your text if this will proliferate hyphenated words).

Another frequent offence is what I call "hopeful substitution". The subject matter or theme is *Obedience*. But we don't have a single poem on *Obedience*, so instead we try to make over a piece on *Insobriety* instead by simply changing the title and one or two words.

For every rule, it seems, there is an excuse. Here are just a few I've encountered over the past twelve years:

Limited to residents of Maine.
"Sure I'm a resident. Do all my shopping in Maine. Live just across the state line."

Must be twenty-five years of age or younger.
"Sure I'm twenty-five. At least I was last year. I just forgot to enter the contest last year, that's all."

Must be original.
"Sure it's original. My dad wrote it."

Limited to 25 lines.
"Sure I can add. You're the one who can't count. Fancy counting a line of only one or two words as a line! One word doesn't make a line. Nor does two or three. You need at least four or five words to make a line. Everyone knows that."

Return postage must be provided.

"I'm sorry there's no return envelope or postage stamp. My son ate them by mistake."

Manuscripts must be thoroughly checked for spelling and grammatical errors.
"Pleasebmn excuse the odd spelling ,.m/.,m,m./,m./,.m/ Oscar keeps jumpinnb on the keys."

Unpublished.
"Published just the once in *The Chesapeake Times Bugle*, average circulation: 155,416. You wouldn't call that *published!*"

No changes are permitted.
"I know I'm a bit of a nuisance but I wonder if you would cancel page 14 in my story, *Ding Dong at Donnybrook*, and substitute the enclosed new page 14 instead and then delete the first seven lines on page 15 (the old page 15) down to the words, 'in my seraglio.' I hope I'm not too much of a nuisance."

Don't put real names on the MS. Use the entry form.
"I don't have an Entry Form, so am sending you my photo instead. That way you'll know it's me if I win a prize."

CHAPTER FOUR

The Right MS for the Right Contest

So you finally find the ideal contest. A reasonably prestigious, regularly offered competition that caters for manuscripts of varied lengths, provides generous cash prizes and perhaps also publication.

This is a good place to mention that publication is not always a desirable criteria. Once a poem or a prose work has been published, that usually puts an end to its contest career. Yet contest organizers usually insist on publishing winning entries themselves. The reason for this is simply that the contest needs to demonstrate to the world at large that it is on the up-and-up. Few readers may agree with the respective worthiness of the entries, but few will doubt that the judging was carried out in an honest if a trifle curious fashion. In other words, it seems more than obvious that a real judge (not the office boy) spent a great deal of time and effort reading and choosing real entries from real entrants (not friends or relatives of the organizers).

However, if you have carried off the $50 Third Prize for the best poem you ever wrote, it does seem a shame that once it has been published in the Podunk Poets' Bulletin, it will never see the light of a printing press again. Not only that, it also becomes ineligible for almost every other poetry event in the world, because just about every contest will not accept "published" work. (The Tom Howard and Margaret Reid Contests are notable exceptions to this general rule).

Anyway, let us assume that, thanks to the good word in Winning Writers or elsewhere, we have finally found a really suitable contest for our endeavors. This is the point, alas, at which 99% of all writers lose out. Having gone to all this trouble to locate a suitable contest that they feel sure will offer them a really good chance of winning, what do they do? They enter a totally inappropriate manuscript.

True, bad choices are often unavoidable. The judge of the contest has not been announced, you have no idea who he or she is, let alone in what direction the judge's tastes lie. This is not good at all. My advice is to avoid all contests in which the judges are not known or if their names will not be published until after the contest closes.

On the very day I'm writing these words, the judge of an extremely popular, highly prestigious, and somewhat expensive poetry contest has just been announced. This is a richly endowed contest, with really tempting cash prizes. It usually attracts over ten thousand entries. Closing date was the day before yesterday. Today, the organizers announce that their record number of entries will be judged by a certain critic who has gone on record with what I consider to be a number of outrageous statements, e.g. that "humor is not a suitable vehicle for poetry." Well, that particular judge's appointment immediately knocks out all the comic and humorous entries. All these poems are instantly discarded. Well, what sort of subjects are deemed suitable for poetry by this prince of critics? "Alzheimer's!" All poems dealing with diseases (the more malevolent the better) straightaway move to the short list.

Now you could rightly argue that as judges are always appointed by organizers, a good guide to subject matter that might be considered appropriate or otherwise can always be obtained by examining past entries. That's definitely true to a certain extent. However, if you don't even have access to successful past entries, all you can do in this instance is submit a varied selection of your best work. Say it's a short story contest, for example. *Open theme.* If it were up to me, I'd send in a literary story, a well-plotted genre piece, a slice-of-life and something a bit unusual. I might even send in a humorous essay as well. At least four or five entries.

Yes, Virginia, it is a sound move to send in more than one entry, so long as you make them <u>varied</u>. Even if the contest specifically targets genre fiction, say crime or mystery, I would send in an Christie-style cozy, a police procedural, a reverse mystery (that's the one where the identity of the killer is revealed from the outset and the mystery is how the thick-headed detective is going to catch up with him), a romantic mystery, an historical mystery, and so on. If the judge was known to be a noted fan of Conan Doyle, I'd be sure to include either a straight or a humorous Sherlock Holmes pastiche. At least I'd be certain the judge would read that particular entry.

Remember too that we authors are often the worst judges of our own work. Hans Anderson thought little of his *Fairy Tales*, Charles Kingsley rated *The Water Babies* far inferior to his *Yeast* or *Hypatia*, and Robert Louis Stevenson regarded *Dr Jekyll and Mr Hyde* as a mere potboiler.

And think of all the fun you'll have trying to guess the judge's selection when you receive a letter from the contest organizer informing you that one of your entries has made the short list! Which one? As often as not, it's the one you'd pick as the runt of the litter. Or the one that took the least time to write and entailed the least amount of research.

It's always possible that you could write the greatest baseball story of all time. Or the greatest scuba diving adventure. But if the judge hates baseball and scuba diving, your pieces don't stand a chance!

However, the best method of tackling competitions where the judges are unknown or unannounced, is, as previously noted, to read the winning entries from last year, and the year before. It is not usually of much value to go back a good deal further because, as also noted, organizers can be replaced. This reading at least will give you a feel for what the current organizers are looking for, even if they employ "guest judges" from year to year. In some cases, the organizing personnel not only does not change from year to year but actually gives the judge a sheet of detailed instructions on just what to look for.

Another essential, of course, is to read the judges' comments on the contests for the last two or three years. When acting as a judge, I was always careful to write up a Report. I don't do it any more because I found that few authors—outside the winning circle—bothered to read it. The winners, of course, are positively anxious to learn what they did so right, but the rest of us are mighty reluctant to see where we went wrong. And often, if we read the adjudicator's comments carefully, we find that we didn't actually make any avoidable mistakes at all. We simply sent in entries the judges didn't like for reasons quite removed from writing quality!

CHAPTER FIVE

A Report on Reports

Here is a fascinating selection of Judges' Reports. (Note especially the words I have underlined):

"It was gratifying to see some imaginative approaches to popular short story themes. In fact, all the prizewinning stories reveal significant imaginative flair. However, certain themes, particularly drug use, were often dealt with in a stereotypical and inauthentic way... Story structure and writing style tended toward the more conventional (as against experimental)... While there was a tendency towards banal dialogue and overuse of dialogue, the main problem area was with endings. Many otherwise good stories were sabotaged by an unconvincing or hurried or heavy-handed ending... Jake was the year's favorite name... We three judges all searched for the same qualities: a mesh of strong characterization, originality, captivating narrative, intellectual depth, and effective writing style."

The author of this Report, Andrea Goldsmith, is one of the nation's top critics. I read her comments very carefully. I didn't just throw the Result Sheets into the nearest rubbish bin and murmur to myself: *How disappointing!* (or words to that effect). *Here's another $5,000 I didn't win! What's the matter with those idiot judges?*

Instead, I hunted out the stories I'd submitted and squared them off against what the judges were actually looking for.

Judges simply don't believe in *open themes* and *all types and genres of stories [or poems] under whatever-number-of-words [or lines] are welcome.* If you don't remember anything else from this handbook, please get it into your head that there is no such animal as an "open" theme. "Open" is easily the most abused word in writing contest literature. Remember again, that as far as writing competitions are concerned, "open" does NOT mean "anything goes." Nor does "unrestricted" mean "unrestricted" or indeed anything like the standard dictionary definition of the word. What these words actually do mean in contest literature is often a matter of conjecture, but I can tell you this: themes are always restricted to some degree. Always! And quite often they are very restricted. Remember, no matter how "open" the theme, there are ALWAYS hidden restrictions of some sort. (I shall return to this abuse of terminology in Chapter Twelve).

In this particular "open-themed" contest, some of these hidden restrictions are now right there for all of us to see. (These restrictions, incidentally, were never publicized but imposed by the judges themselves after the contest had closed). Drugs, for example. Any and all stories about "drug use" went straight into the reject pile.

How can I say that, Virginia argues? All that the three judges say in their combined report is that *certain themes, particularly drug use, were often dealt with in stereotypical and inauthentic way*. The judges don't say, hotly argues Virginia, that ALL stories about drugs were rejected.

Oh, yes, they do, Virginia! This was a *combined* report. Believe me, judges are very pernickety and quarrelsome people. They probably spent more time arguing through every word in their combined report than they did in actually judging the entries. You've got to read these majority reports very scrupulously, between the lines. If there was just ONE exception, you can bet your bottom dollar one of these cross-all-the-tees judges would have insisted on mentioning it. I know! I've sat on committees of judges. It's often taken us more time, more energy, more fights to write the blessed report than anything else!

And yet after all this time, energy and labor, entrants get the report, they glance at it, they see they didn't win anything and they just throw it away!

It's incredible, but true! How many Judges' Reports have you read lately, line by line, word by word, thought by thought? (I mean, of course, those reports in which your name was, unaccountably, not mentioned).

Okay, now that I've discussed ONE thing the judges didn't want, what were they looking for?

This particular set of judges wanted "strong characterization, a convincingly logical, satisfying ending, originality (especially in the use of an imaginative, experimental style and structure), captivating narrative, intellectual depth, and effective writing style." A hard ask. If your story missed out on just one of these qualities, you simply weren't in the running.

But, as I've said, even more fascinating are revelations as to what the judges didn't want: stories with heavy-handed endings, too much dialogue, banal dialogue, too little or no experimentation. Also on the outer: stories about drug misuse, and (would you believe?) plots with any characters named "Jake".

See, I told you judges were a highly eccentric lot. It's not what you like that wins competitions. It's not even good solid writing that guarantees entry to the winners' circle. It's simply an entry that positively panders to the judges' tastes! And if you don't know what those tastes are, your chances of winning a major prize are minimal.

As to why my own stories hit the instant reject button, I didn't have to look any further than *too much dialogue*. I'm not really a short story writer. My background is solidly in journalism. And when it comes to fiction, I'm a playwright in disguise. The first award I ever won—at the age of eighteen—was Fourth Prize in a One-Act Play Competition sponsored by the Federal Government. This competition attracted hundreds of entries from professional writers all over the country, including our most acclaimed playwrights (who took out prizes one, two, and three).

I came fourth. Eighteen years old. Up there with the greatest of them. Playwrights who are household names even today.

Anyway, I think it's true to say I use a lot of dialogue in my fiction. I try my hardest to make that dialogue interesting, snappy, amusing, witty, sharp, piquant, colloquial and revealingly in character. I also rely principally on dialogue to fulfill other functions like advancing the plot, imparting necessary background information, and especially creating atmosphere and suspense.

But no matter how apt it is, you can't get away from the fact that it's dialogue. Pages and pages of the stuff.

I confess I also have a weakness for a series of monosyllabic replies. (It's a hark-back to my youth. I love W.S. Gilbert!). Take this exchange between Merryll "Merry" Manning (an ex-cop playing nursemaid to a bunch of street kids) and Sergeant Quist of the Copper Coast police in my book, *Merryll Manning: Fast Times in Paradise*. Quist has enlisted Merryll's help to find a snobby, intellectually pretentious, teenage gang leader named Jason who didn't turn up (as required by his parole conditions) for Pastor Hi's Sunday sermon. Manning is speaking:

"Let's approach this pipsqueak problem illogically, Dr Watson. Where's the last place in Paradise you'd expect this devil's disciple to be found?"

Quist's expression changed to blank.

"Think, Dr Watson, think! The last place in Paradise?"

"Morgue."

"No. That's where we all expect him to end up. Thinking cap's awry, Dr Watson. I'll give you a clue. We're hunting high and low for all the eyes and ears of Paradise."

Screaming all manner of coarse blasphemies and

expletives, the enraged Quist kicked in the advertising panel of an innocent street bin.

"You forget, Quist. Sunday's my day off. I'm only obliged to be nice to you, Mondays to Fridays. Now, do you want help or not? Okay, let's play the game. Where were we? The last place, Quist?"

"Library."

"Getting warmer, but closed Sundays."

"Surf?"

"Cold."

"Beach?"

"Freezing."

"Football?"

"Warm."

"Sport?"

"Less warm."

"Shops?"

"Nope."

"Movies?"

"Not open."

"Art gallery?"

"More like it, but no."

"Cab?"

"Sizzling, but too late."

"Jesus, Merry!"

"Got it in twelve, Quist! Watson himself couldn't have done any better. Your next question is: What church?"

"Church? Church? Back at Pastor Hi's," answered Quist hopefully.

"Come off it! Why do you think Hi roused us out to go looking for the little blighter?"

"Hiding?"

I shook my head. "Dining."

"Café?"

"Church, remember, Watson. Church."

"Wesley?"

"Good thinking, but no. Too close. He wouldn't need a cab."

"Father Lowe?"

I nodded.

"What the hell's he doin' there?"

"Having lunch."

Quist stared at me for a full ten seconds before the penny dropped. "Hell, Merry! You knew all the flamin' time!"

As I said, all the stories I submitted depended on far "too much dialogue" in the opinion of this particular bunch of critics. What to do?

Well, a few months later, I spotted one of these same judges listed at another comp. So I sent in a story called "Wright and Wrong" which has no dialogue at all! None! Not only did this effort make the final short list, but it has now been published in the University's anthology.

Then I sent the same story off to another of our esteemed places of learning. One of the few comps, in fact, which will accept already published material. I'm not about to tell you the name of this one because (surprise! surprise!) they hated the story.

[Three prestigious literary competitions that will accept (under certain not-too-rigorous conditions) previously published copy are The Tom Howard Short Story, Essay and Prose Contest, The Margaret Reid Prize for Traditional Verse, and the Tom Howard Poetry Contest (all of which I judge. A free plug for myself! But look at all the tips I'm giving you!)]

However, as far as me and mine are concerned, I would certainly not agree that using "too much dialogue" was in any way a fault—unless, of course, that dialogue came across as banal, ordinary, dull, pointless chatter which served no purpose other than to fill up three or four pages.

I do make an effort to keep in mind that a short story is not a play. I try to vary slabs of dialogue with imaginative, perspicacious descriptions of scenery and places (though I avoid detailing all the physical features of my characters). Would you believe that this admirable habit put me in dutch with another judge who wrote in her comments on the winning story: "Every word is made to count in the <u>minimal</u> descriptions of surroundings." That certainly didn't apply to my entries. On the other hand, I fully endorse her other comment: "The winning entry aroused my interest in <u>the very first sentence</u>."

CHAPTER SIX

More Contest Reports

One year, I won The Hills Library Prize. The very next year, I entered again, but only carried off a Commended certificate. Never mind, the adjudicators' comments were most interesting. I reprint them here in full:

"When reading these short stories, the judges looked for a number of attributes—firstly we looked for a good story that contained <u>effective use of language, conflict and resolution, atmosphere and believability.</u> A number of good stories—interesting, entertaining stories—were let down by the absence of an ending. They left the reader dangling or else had an ending that let the story down. The main stories managed to provide both an entertaining story and an effective ending.

"We read the entries not once, but many times. The decision to select the winners proved difficult because there were a large number of stories worthy of merit. However, after <u>several readings,</u> the main prizewinners emerged through their immediate and believable character portrayals, a story structure that was coherent, and language that added to the quality of the story. The prizewinning stories maintained their effectiveness through several readings and kept their entertainment value because they relied not simply on the story but on the elegance and appropriateness of the language used.

"Again we were disappointed in the number of entries that contained spelling errors <u>and corrections.</u> It is a simple matter to attend to these types of details to give your entry <u>the best possible chance in a competition.</u>"

I agree entirely with the judges, and would draw

your special attention to the words *several times* and *several readings*. I'm sure that all of us expect judges to read our stories not just once, but three or even four times. I do several readings myself when weighing entries in the Tom Howard Contests. Last year, however, I noticed a peculiar aberration. A story I had selected as a possible first prizewinner, moved further and further away from the winners' circle the more times I read it. I wondered why. Then I realized that part of its impact on a first reading was due to its wonderfully shattering surprise ending. A perfectly logical ending, and one I should have expected. But it never occurred to me initially, I was so swept up by the onward pace of the story itself. Unfortunately, on a second reading, the ending no longer held any shock at all, and the story was therefore robbed of a lot of its drama.

So what do we learn from this? Avoid stories with surprise endings unless, of course, specifically asked, and unless you can counterbalance the ending with elegance and style. Henry James' *Washington Square* is a superb example of a story with a shattering ending that can yet be read over and over because of its brilliantly lifelike yet sympathetic characterizations, its moody and broodingly ingrown atmosphere, and its totally captivating style.

I'm sure all of us have had enough of short stories for the moment. All you poets are eagerly waiting in the wings. So here's a very informative report (one of the best I've read) from Jennifer Harrison, the sole judge of the 2003 National Poetry Competition:

"What a competition! 687 poems read over a two-week period… Rather than talk at length about the qualities of the prize winners, I prefer to say something about the judging process…

"The first reading of the poems was the easiest. Often, it quickly became clear whether a poet had control of their material. Poems that drooped by the wayside at this stage were clichéd, grammatically inept, flowery, unnecessarily indulgent, rhyming doggerel, or lacking musicality.

"Harsh, perhaps, but true.

"It's worth mentioning that particular categories of poems tended to survive this first read: 1. the 'language poem'; 2. the highly original, eccentric poem; and 3. the poem that challenges genre.

"These three 'radical' categories of poems caught my attention and often demanded a second or third reading. Overall, though, I think they are disadvantaged in the context of a competition. After reading so many poems, I found myself hungry for writing that was clear and concise; writing that was original yet had emotional resonance. Poems that challenge the syntax of poetry have to be good to survive. Other poems that subvert the structures and concepts of language itself require the author's other writing to fully comprehend the interface that the poet is working. Decontextualized, they may, and often do, lose some of their power.

"I read every submitted poem twice and in that process the 687 poems were culled to 50, a fairly drastic diminution. I also kept a pile of 30 'maybes' for consideration. I returned to certain poems, thought about them and read them aloud. Poems falter at this stage because of more aesthetic considerations: if the subject matter is tired; if I feel the poet hasn't challenged me enough. Problems with flow and tone become significant. A poem may have been progressing fabulously and then: an awkward image, flat melody, a nondescript or overworked finish.

"The final 30 poems lived with me for a week. At this stage, personal taste is the only arbiter. The poems by now have strong voices. The poets are brave. The poems, like gemstones, are often flawed but have originality and depth. These are qualities I admire. This is the point where the judge's personal taste takes over. From the 30 short-listed, a number of fine poems that did not win gongs from me, might have succeeded had someone else been judging the competition. I chose poems that intrigued me. No one form or genre predominated, but I like contradictions...

"Reading back over what I've written, words such as 'cull', 'cut', 'fall', 'falter' in relation to the judging process appear despotic and quite ruthless. I'm afraid it is so. The poems that shine through have been a delight."

The sensitivity Jennifer Harrison brought to bear on all the entries, serves us a model to all judges. It is not, however, my method. Nor is it the stratagem employed by most adjudicators. I'm afraid the sheer volume of entries tends to make us impose arbitrary rules which I'm sure the contest organizers never thought of, let alone wished to apply.

For an extreme example of the opposite approach, I would like to cite U.A. Fanthorpe, the 2003 judge of the Bridport Prize (which is surely one of the world's most prestigious open-to-all-comers poetry contests, although it will, as previously noted, accept only hard copy entries):

"It is discreditable to admit this, but in the early stages I longed for poems for the NO pile... {A poem} will be typed, of course, and not all in capitals; it will use upper and lower case in the normal way; and where a space is usual, it will have a space. It will probably be on white paper or possibly blue, but almost certainly not pink. It will not be decorated with ornamental scrollwork in colored ink...

"I like the Bridport method of adjudicating. One person judges the whole lot. [Over 5,000 entries were received in 2003]. It makes for a very heavy load, but it avoids the kind of horse-trading I've met in three-judge competitions which can result in the top prize going to a compromise candidate which no-one thinks is the best."

Miss Fanthorpe selected the winning poems on the basis that "they read aloud well" and were "consistent".

"There were some splendid comic poems," she concedes, "but it is hard to prefer them to the more somber poems about Alzheimer's, suicide or loss."

To be fair, Miss Fanthorpe is quoting another critic about the colored paper. I'm sure that she herself threw blue-papered poems into the rubbish pile with as much alacrity as she disposed of the pink.

I agree that poems must be "consistent". There must be a relationship between form and content. But I would never reject a poem simply because it used lower-case personal pronouns or misused spacing. If the poem's point of view was that of a backward, illiterate no-hoper then the lower-case pronouns and other grammatical solecisms become entirely appropriate. And if the poem rejoiced in the title, "Everything Blue", I would not object to blue paper. In fact, I'd be delighted.

Yet for all the "i"s that don't have it and all the multihued stationery that fails to impress, in the main I believe Miss Fanthorpe is on the right track. Just one of her points, however, I do find really hard to swallow, namely her difficulty in ranking a splendid comic poem above a somber piece about Alzheimer's Disease.

I feel there is far too much critical adulation these days (particularly from university and literary circles) directed towards poems that deal with unromantic, distressing and even ugly subjects.

In my opinion, poetry by its very nature does not provide a vehicle to invoke the unspeakable. I tell you right now, send me a poem about leprosy, cancer or any other hideous disease and that poem is heading straight for the recycle bin.

This does not mean that poetry should necessarily be uplifting. I reject that concept also. A poem is heightened prose. It is prose that has been reworked (through the imaginative use of "poetic license") to form a striking or appealing pattern. That pattern can be metrical, musical, thematic, artistic, linear, subliminal, visual, repetitive, imagistic or any combination of such qualities. Its themes will transcend love and beauty, humor and life, Nature and death.

The ideal poem will combine cadence with imagery. In other words, it will please the ear as well as the eye. (Prose should do this too, but in a much more subtle way).

Just one more poetry report:

"While a few entries showed no relevance to the set theme, most managed to obey the requirement without obvious laboring of the point. Many pieces were well written and employed apt imagery, but had little to distinguish them from each other. In a competition environment, your entry must stand out to have a chance."

One of the longest reports I received was written by Brett D'Arcy, judge of the 2003 Katharine Susannah Prichard Short Fiction Awards. I extract just one of his points: "It is my personal opinion that in these increasingly mean-spirited times in which the dispossessed and marginalized in our society are being squeezed within an inch of their economic lives, there is less and less room for purely decorative prose."

Oh, dear! This brings us back to the old argument that I thought Oscar Wilde scotched forever back in 1891 when he wrote in *The Critic as Artist*: "It is through Art, and through Art only, that we can realize our perfection; through Art, and through Art only, that we can shield ourselves from the sordid perils of actual existence."

When he rejects purely decorative prose, Mr D'Arcy rejects some of the greatest writers in the English language: Jerome K. Jerome, Edgar Allan Poe, Robert Louis Stevenson, Sherwood Anderson, Scott Fitzgerald, Washington Irving, A.A. Milne, Ambrose Bierce, Mark Twain, Arnold Bennett, Stephen Leacock, Hal Porter, O.

Henry... the list is endless. Much as I admire John Steinbeck, I don't want to spend my life in the environs of *The Grapes of Wrath* nor *Of Mice and Men*.

However, Mr D'Arcy continues with one really important observation for which he deserves a hearty clap on the back: "As financial considerations continue to take precedence over social ones and political initiatives take an increasingly heartless right-wing tack across the nation... I find myself drawn to those stories which seek to make a difference. Given Katharine Susannah Prichard's political endeavor and social work and the ethical nature of many of her books... this criteria would seem to be wholly appropriate."

Mr D'Arcy is the first and only adjudicator I've ever encountered who has given any weight whatever to the title of the competition he is judging.

It always annoys me that organizers often name their competitions after famous authors and books and then completely ignore all the qualities those authors stand for. The title of a contest is often nothing more than a red herring designed to separate gullible writers from their entry fees. So if you hear of a contest that offers itself as the Sherwood Anderson Short Story Award, it's wrong to assume the organizers are seeking stories about loners and grotesques, written in a charmingly lucid, yet thoroughly sympathetic style. Nothing could be further from the truth. The winning piece will probably feature a graphic account of unhygienic practices in a salmon cannery.

CHAPTER SEVEN

Know Your Judge

Yes, Virginia, although the actual name of the competition may be wholly irrelevant, our chances of success do improve dramatically if the identity of the judge is revealed in big bold letters on the entry form. Provided we take the trouble to find out something about the judge before rushing in our entries.

Speaking of *rushing*, a good tip here is not to rush your entry in at the last moment if you can possibly help it. Early submissions in some contests enjoy a distinct advantage. The Tom Howard Contest, which I judge, is an excellent example of this, because I read the entries as they come in. When the contest opens, I receive approximately one a day. I have plenty of time to read that story, to enjoy it, to savor it, to appreciate it. I really look forward to the one or two stories that arrive almost daily on my desk via snail or email. These early entries then set the standard. If, for instance, I select *Rainbow Roundabout* by Xavier Xerxes as a possible winner, I will say to myself when judging subsequent entries: "Yes, that was a fine story I just read by Marjorie M. Montague. But is it as intriguing, as moving, as gripping as *Rainbow Roundabout* by Xavier Xerxes?"

Two other advantages that early submissions have are that the judge is then actually looking for worthwhile entries, and is consequently less inclined to reject stories or poems for minor or even frivolous faults (like poor lay-out or the use of staples for binding instead of clips). At this stage, the judge needs to build up his list of potential winners. There's nothing worse than a contest in which prizes are not awarded because entries failed to attain a sufficiently high standard. Most judges will bend over backwards to excuse minor faults in the early stages of a competition.

Needless to say, by the time the deadline draws near and twenty or thirty manuscripts pile up on my desk every day, I simply don't have the time to give them all the really close-close inspection they deserve. What's more, I'm now seeking excuses to send entries into the reject basket. True, a story that's out of the box will always win over my heart: "That was certainly a wonderful story by Elaine Edwards. Is it as brilliant as *Rainbow Roundabout*? Yes, I have to admit it's even better!"

Now let me speak about myself in the third person and pretend that I'm a potential entrant to the Tom Howard Short Story Contest. I know nothing about the judge. So the first thing I do is look up his biography. I see that mystery novels are one of his specialties.

At this point, I would seriously consider writing and submitting mystery or crime, if I thought I possessed any aptitude for this genre.

On the other hand, this piece of knowledge also works in reverse. If the judge is an expert on writing detective stories, maybe it's not a good idea to let him read my less professional or less polished efforts. Maybe I should send him a little romance where his standards are not so high. Hmmm.

I also notice that Reid's a film critic. I'm a bit of a fan of the old movies too. So maybe if I can formulate a story with a movie background, chances are that good old John Howard Reid will read it with great interest.

Who was that actor in that old, old movie set in a gambling den in some weird place which this girl was trying to escape from? You know the one I mean. There was a song in that movie called "Time Goes By". Hmmm.

Perhaps I don't know enough about old movies after all. So back to the bio. John Howard Reid also has a soft spot for country clubs. Was once a director in fact. Another no-

no. What I know about country clubs you could write on the back of a traffic ticket.

Okay! So none of Reid's reported interests match my own. But I do have another ace up my sleeve. My next best bet is to read a few stories by John Howard Reid to get a handle on other subjects he writes about. Not only will I get some inkling as to the type of stories he favors, but also the style of prose he uses.

Some of you will object that I'm going about this *all wrong*. You remind me that the rules of the competition say *Open theme*.

That proviso never means what it says. Not in <u>any</u> creative writing contest. What it actually spells out is the very opposite: *If you expect to win a prize, theme must be on the judge's wavelength!*

So know your judge. Read some of his or her work. Find out something about him or her. Don't fall into the trap that I *fell* into the other day. The judge of the comp was spelt out in big letters. But I took no notice. *Never heard of her*, I said. Never bothered to look her up. Sent in three top-class stories. Turns out she's one of these literary types. She doesn't want a story with a beginning, a middle and an end. She doesn't even want a story with a grab-you-right-from-the-start beginning, a slam-bang middle and a knock-your-socks-off finish. In fact, she loathes such stories. What she'll be handing out prizes for are waffly pieces about bereft old ladies left to rot in rundown nursing homes. Or even worse, hospital operations that went awry, described in grisly, ghastly detail.

Summary: *Know your judge. Read at least a little of his or her work.*

CHAPTER EIGHT

Choose Your Contest

As previously noted, many writing contests, even a few of the most prestigious, do not announce their judge or judges in advance. For would-be-successful authors, that's a double disadvantage. Firstly, there's a possibility that a contest with an anonymous or yet-to-be-appointed adjudicator could be a scam. Later in this chapter, I'll discuss scam and bogus competitions and how to recognize them. Secondly, the author is forced to fly blind. Sometimes, as already discussed, we are given an opportunity to look up some previous prizewinners; but, just as often, even this option is either not available at all or available at a price we're unwilling to pay. And in any event, if the judges change from year to year, aside from getting a very broad inkling or two, what's the point?

So here are my pointers for flying blind in Short Story and Poetry Contests:

Short Stories: I've already pointed out that *Open theme* usually means anything but. The first thing the novice contestant must realize is that, speaking generally, there are two vastly different types of stories that competitions seek. Firstly, we have the *literary* type of story. Be warned! Contests run or sponsored by colleges, universities, student bodies and so-called "small presses" are invariably seeking *literature*. On the one hand, experimentation is encouraged. On the other, it is expected that contributors will toe the current academic lines, especially in regard to content. Characters are often sleazy, or at best, lower class. Descriptions often dwell on unsavory aspects of the milieu these characters inhabit; and the stories seem to get nowhere. The approach is both Freudian and nihilistic. In other words, the stories are deliberately designed to express values rejected or ignored by *popular* storytellers.

Popular Stories are generally sought by competitions that seek to emulate the fiction formerly published in magazines like *Esquire* or *The Saturday Evening Post*. Often the smaller and regional writers' clubs and associations will sponsor contests for such stories that appeal to general readers rather than a few cloistered university academics.

Another clear pointer to the type of story that a particular contest is actually seeking is offered by that magic word, *publication*. In some countries and in many states, a publisher is obliged to exercise a certain amount of caution regarding the content of books and magazines that are offered for sale in locations frequented by children or that are likely to be stocked by school libraries.

Speaking for the Tom Howard Short Story Contest, I can assure you that the anthology of winning stories is offered for sale everywhere. As a consequence, any story that is centered on *Adults Only* themes will be rejected. A winning story that incorporates unacceptable words or sentences will be censored.

However, although my leaning is towards the spellbindingly-crafted *popular story*, I will not reject *literature* if it engages my interest or attention. In other words, *open theme* in the Tom Howard Contest really means just that. The only proviso is that the stories must be suitable in subject matter and presentation for a reasonably broadminded cross-section of the community, as well as jaded university dons.

Poems. Here we have not only two distinct divides between *university poetry* and *popular poetry* but between *free verse* and *traditional verse*. Whilst it's true that university poetry always employs various forms of both

43

free verse and prose, popular poetry can only be couched in either free verse or traditional. Until the last decade, the popular poem tended to favor traditional versification in rhyme and/or meter, but now free verse well and truly has the upper hand.

So, when entering poetry contests here are some points to remember:

1. Don't bother to submit traditional verse (no matter how superbly crafted or devastatingly original) to university journals, literary reviews, small press magazines, and publications sponsored by national or urban poetry societies unless the rules state *specifically* that traditional poetry entries are welcome. The only exception to this rule is that *some* university-type organizations accept *humorous* verse laid out in traditional forms.

2. University poetry usually favors quirky punctuation (the personal pronoun in lower case, an ampersand symbol instead of "and") and ghastly subject matter. If you hate using the shift key on your keyboard and you're a whiz at describing the onslaught of some hideous disease, you've got it made.

3. However, there is at least one development on the academic poetry front that I heartily endorse. This is the creation called a prose poem or "storoem". (Hate the name, but love the idea). Basically it's a short story or prose piece that is often (though not always) set out in poetry-type lines. To my mind, this method allows the writer to better express what she or he wants to say, because the storyteller/poet manages to seamlessly emphasize certain words or phrases without recourse to the crudely primitive technique of underlining.

4. If you prefer to write in free verse but are not really interested in storoems or the inner workings of sewerage treatment plants or a step-by-step analysis of post-mortem procedures at the city morgue, your best bets lie in the contests run by small but enthusiastic writers' groups. True,

these are very small-scale affairs with very modest prizes, but they are better than nothing. One problem here is that modest contests can only afford to pay modest fees to their judges and they sometimes engage real ratbags. My local poetry group fell into this trap. It's a large group that runs a quite respectable competition every two years, a competition so well established it's actually supported by a small grant from local government. The average age of members would certainly be in the fifties or sixties. While free verse is encouraged, the excesses of current university cliques are definitely frowned upon. Unfortunately, the judge turned out to be one of these academic radicals. Rejecting every single one of the poems submitted by society members, he insisted on awarding prizes to "verse" that simply did not qualify. And I do mean *not qualify*. Although the rules clearly stated that the poem was to be unpublished, the judge chose to give the grand prize to a piece that had already appeared in print, not once, but twice! (While thankfully uncommon, such blatant disregard of the rules is manifestly unfair to all other contestants, most of whom would certainly have submitted a published poem if the rules had not prevented this. Unfortunately, you can't argue with judges. They're a law unto themselves).

That is a worst case scenario, but I have struck quite intelligent adjudicators who insisted on such outmoded distinctions as rhyming verse versus free verse. I don't see any reason why free verse can't or shouldn't rhyme. But to some adjudicators, rhyming verse must always be categorized as traditional verse, and judged as such. Well! There go all my entries into the reject basket! Sometimes, I use rhymes for emphasis and effect, but I rarely employ traditional meters. So the judge hands me back my work with the comment: "Good ideas, imaginative imagery, but your verses don't scan!"

"They're not meant to," I reply.

They take no notice. "You need to go to a Poetry

Workshop," they advise.

Me! Who's won a Third Prize in a prestigious National Poetry Contest, and Highly Commended certificates galore!

5. Although derided and scorned by the academic establishment, traditional verse is still not only very much alive, but exceptionally healthy. You'll find plenty of outlets. Too many, in fact. Which brings us to –

Scams. Astoundingly, scam contests have found a receptive home on the Internet. Almost all these scam electronic sites encourage traditional poetry – and they have found tens of thousands of takers. Incredible but true! Here's how the scam works. Budding poets are encouraged by fabulous cash prizes and free entry to send off small snippets (usually no more than twenty lines) of doggerel. They then receive a letter from the organizer praising their puerile efforts to the skies and offering to publish this junk in a handsomely bound Anthology. No charge for publication, but of course you will want to buy this fabulously beautiful book featuring your own personal page of trash for a ridiculous price. And why not buy copies for all your friends, relatives and heirs? You're a poet, my daughter!

CHAPTER NINE

Contest Don'ts

Beware of:

1. Free poetry contests that are not contests. They are in fact draws or lotteries. The winning entries are drawn at random. Winning one of these "contests" will certainly put a bit of money in your bank, but it's worth less than zilch in prestige. However, it's important to note that not *all* free contests are scams. There are some legitimate ones out there. You'll find a list of these legits at *Winning Writers*, a site I heartily recommend. One of the features of a scam contest that writers (especially novice writers) find attractive is that it seems so simple to enter. No pages of complicated rules to scan (admittedly there are writers who are congenitally unable to read rules anyway, but that's another story). Just type (or paste) your poem into the on-line form and press "Submit". Unfortunately, the easier a contest is to enter, the more likely that it is not a "contest" at all, just a lucky dip.

2. Allied with the free contest is the "contest mill" offered on some Internet sites on such a regular monthly (or even weekly) basis that little if any time is allowed for judging. I suspect that most of these "contests" also select winners at random. (A judging variation that is often used is to select entries at random but reject obvious rubbish until entries that are at least halfway presentable make the draw). Like the lottery "contests", winning one of these may put a small dollop of money in your pocket or some useless merchandise (like a T-shirt) in your hand, but as a writing credit, it rates less than zero.

3. Contests that promise a king's ransom in cash prizes, all blocked out in great big bold type. Hidden in tiny print

in two and a half pages of Rules, you'll often find a para that states: "Prizes will be reduced pro rata if less than 500 (or somesuch ridiculously high number) entries are received." Beware!

4. Conversely, give a wide berth to contests where the entry fees seem disproportionately high, compared to the prizes. If the contest is organized by your local writers' group, I'd expect a $5 entry fee to give me access to at least a $100 prize. Speaking generally, however, I'd want the ratio to equal (or be greater) than one to a hundred. So, if the fee were ten dollars, I'd want the total cash distribution to add up to at least one thousand dollars. If the fee were fifteen dollars, I'd expect to see at least fifteen hundred in prize money.

5. Be wary of new contests offering fabulous sums. Even if they are sponsored by big organizations, contests rarely cover their expenses for their first five or six years. A contest that's been running for five years or more may possibly be more of a lottery than a genuine contest, but at least you can be reasonably sure that someone somewhere is going to collect a pile of dough. My eye was recently attracted to an online contest for a novel that offered cash prizes totaling $100,000 for an $85 entry fee. Sounds like a real good deal. So I downloaded a copy of the rules. All four pages of them. Buried in this persiflage was the following statement: "In the event an insufficient number of entries are received, Wrippoff Books reserves the right to cancel the Competition and shall be under no obligation to award the prizes, but will refund $40 of the [$85] Registration Fee to the author's Wrippoff account." You will notice that no exact number is specified to qualify the word "insufficient".

6. This is just a personal gripe and it is NOT an indication of a scam, but one literary "event" that really irritates me is a contest that provides just ONE prize. Usually this ONE single prize is one thousand dollars

48

(because that's the limit imposed by Poets and Writers Magazine and other agents for *listing* the contest – which is crazy. You could have a contest that gave away a hundred prizes of $999, totaling $99,900 in cash, but Poets and Writers would refuse to list it because your First Prize is less than $1,000. It doesn't matter a hoot to Poets and Writers if your First Prize is your only prize so long as it's at least $1,000! Crazy!). Anyway, what I don't like about this competition, purely from a contestant's point of view, is the odds. If the contest scores five hundred entries, my chance of winning is only one in five hundred. Fat chance! Even Steinbeck or Faulkner would balk at those odds. However, if two prizes are awarded, my prospects increase to one in two fifty. If five prizes are awarded, I then have one chance in a hundred. If ten prizes, one chance in fifty. At this point, I can always better the odds if I submit multiple entries. For two entries, I have now one chance in twenty-five. And with five entries, I progress to one chance in ten. Whilst I hope and pray that my work is judged on its merits, I also like to know that the odds are in my favor and that, mathematically at least, I have a reasonable expectation of making the winner's circle.

7. Another contest that I don't look upon with favor, though it's often most definitely not a scam, is the "publisher's reward". As the name implies, this competition is usually financed by publishers (both legitimate and vanity presses) and sometimes by literary agents, writing coaches and manuscript appraisal services. It works like this: The organizer asks for submissions for which he charges a fairly high reading fee (usually around $50). The prize, however, is not cash, but publication. In many cases, the publisher is legitimate, and in this instance the system can certainly work to the writer's advantage. His work accepted by a major house, he recoups his $50 ten thousand times over and becomes an instant success. If the publisher is a vanity press, however, all the author receives

are a few copies (usually around ten or twenty) of his book. Even worse, all the entrants (including the winner) are badgered by the vanity press into shelling out thousands of dollars to have their books "published". Similarly, the agents, coaches and manuscript doctors also send entrants a deluge of illusionary inducements to part with their savings. So beware! When entering this type of contest, be sure to ascertain the primary business of the promoter. If the organizer is a legitimate publisher, you could be the next Dan Brown. On the other hand, you could end up in the poor house.

CHAPTER TEN

Submitting Your Manuscript

The three basic methods used to forward submissions to contests are:

1. Snail mail. Would you believe, many of the world's best-known contests still <u>insist</u> on this method of delivery, though changes are slowly on the way.

2. Electronic: Email and/or online. Many contests, including most of the scams, use this method <u>exclusively</u>.

3. Both. This alternative was gradually becoming more widespread until a few years ago. Now, however, there is feeling among some judges that physically handling entries rather than reading them via a computer, has a number of advantages, particularly for contests in which the decision rests with a three-member team. The judges are not staring at computer screens and sending off emails to each other, but are interacting face-to-face with the relevant entries right in their hands. The disadvantage, of course, is that if the contest headquarters are located in New York and the judges reside in L.A., Chicago and Calgary, the contest is forced to pay out considerable traveling and hotel expenses, in addition to the normal judges' fees. The end result is less money in the prize pool. Which is why some very well-known contests with celebrity judges, medium-range entry fees, and a large number of entrants, pay out comparatively modest prizes.

As for the Tom Howard Prose and Poetry Contests, as well as the Margaret Reid Prize for Traditional Verse, these three competitions have always accepted entries both electronically and through traditional post. Of course, electronic access didn't exist for the first eight years of the Prose Contest. The first year this alternative was offered, that is for Contest Number Nine, a total of only a mere 35 entries were received electronically (compared to more than fifteen times that number by regular post). The second year, electronic entries more than quadrupled, but still represented only a small fraction of the total. In 2004, however, more than a third of the submissions were received by email or posted online. In 2006, the breakdown was close to ninety per cent electronic and only ten per cent regular mail. Why this sudden explosion in 2006? Simply because writers worldwide suddenly, if belatedly realized, that electronic submission does away with national boundaries. In previous years, the Tom Howard Contests had received entries exclusively from writers in the USA, Canada, Australia and New Zealand. In 2006, for the first time, came entrants from England, France, India, Mexico, Poland, Germany, Spain, Sweden, Egypt, Czechoslovakia, Hungary, Switzerland, and South Africa.

But then a very peculiar thing happened. Snail mail staged a comeback. Every year the proportion increased. It is now around half and half. Why this sudden reversal? The simple answer: Formatting. No amount of scientific effort has managed to get the bugs out of email transmission (if anything, electronic mangling is worse!) and many writers are understandably upset when they see what cyberspace has done to their carefully laid-out work.

Naturally the Tom Howard judges have revised their strategy to accommodate this problem. All entries are judged on the same field and therefore the judges give no consideration whatever to formatting or lay-out.

So what to do if your contest offers alternative choices of submission? The easy solution of course is always to use email or online upload. No more printing out pages and cover sheets and stapling them together, then finding an envelope of suitable size and carting the lot off to the post office. But there are disadvantages:

The worst thing that can happen, of course, is that your

entry may not be received at all. There is actually a much greater chance of your work being lost in cyberspace than through the regular mail. In the seventeen years of the Tom Howard Contest, I've only known of two entries that went astray in the old-fashioned mail. There may be others of course, but I only <u>know</u> of these two. On the other hand, in the nine years of electronic submissions, I <u>know</u> of five. As you can see, loss is still an extremely outside chance, no matter what service is used, but it's worth considering. *Always keep a back-up hard copy of your work!*

The second worst thing that can happen is that your entry is not received intact. While this rates as only a remote possibility in the regular mail service, we all know that in electronic transmissions this sort of thing happens at least five per cent of the time. How is it that junk mail and advertising promos always arrive letter perfect, but our stories and poems are occasionally truncated and often re-set? Our carefully selected *Italics* suddenly become <u>Roman</u>, and our line breaks and our margins either disappear completely or suddenly gulf wide—right in the middle of a paragraph. The size of our fonts are also subject to alterations and even the fonts themselves are sometimes changed. Our stories, in short, are often not presented to the judge in the format we chose. Fortunately these problems can be rectified during the publication process (that is, if the particular contest offers publication), but they are still a nuisance.

Fortunately, as noted, the Tom Howard and Margaret Reid judges no longer take format or lay-out into their deliberations; but this enlightened approach does not necessarily apply to other contests.

My preferred method as a contestant is to use snail mail (if it's an available option) within my home country, and always online submission overseas, unless, of course, only postal mail entry is offered. The online form at least allows you to correct format errors after pasting—even if some or all of your corrections do not take permanent hold.

When using hard copy for those contests that insist upon such submissions, neat presentation is a <u>must</u>. Many competitions insist on double spacing and all sorts of fuddy-duddy requirements like width of margins, methods of binding and even the size and type of fonts. I once predicted that this disadvantage, coupled with postage and enveloping, would inevitably drive more and more contestants to use electronic alternatives. This has not happened. In fact, the reverse has taken place.

I have in front of me a long article about the vital importance of formatting entries from Peter Hanbury, a very respected critic and judge. Mind you, I agree entirely with what Peter says. The problem is, as I've noted above, that as far as I'm concerned, the good old internet has thrown formatting out the window. If you are judging a contest that accepts both electronic and hard copy submissions, it's not fair to take formatting into account.

However, getting back to hard copy tacks, there's no arguing with Peter's observation that, whether deliberately or though sheer carelessness, some entrants do make things difficult for themselves. It's very off-putting for a judge to be suddenly confronted with a mass of seemingly solid type. Personally, I don't mind single spacing, provided you retain a double space between paragraphs. And I'm happy to read any font, but I prefer Garamond or Times Roman. This is Times Roman. It rates as the default font in most computer programs because it's simply the easiest to read. This is 12 point, which I think you'll agree is not too large, not too small, but just right.

CHAPTER ELEVEN

The Judging Process

First, I'll let you in the actual physical process and then we'll discuss exactly what most judges are looking for.

When the contest organizer receives your entries (by whatever means they're delivered), he either keeps them all secure until the contest closes or sends them weekly, monthly and sometimes even as received, to the judge. Normally, the second option is used when the judge is permanently associated with this particular award, the first when the judge is a "guest".

In the Tom Howard Contests, all entries are read by Professor Konrad, the associate judge, as received. But this is not usually the case with most other literary competitions where submissions undergo as many as three or four preliminary sortings, before the "name" judge or judges deliver a final verdict. Volunteers are often engaged for the first cull. They are instructed to eliminate all entries that require extensive editorial work. Poor grammar, inveterately incorrect spelling and entries that blatantly disregard the competition's rules (especially in regard to length) or have no return addresses and no accompanying entry fees, all fall into this category. Also culled at this point are all manuscripts that don't *look* professional. Coffee-stained cover sheets and all those dog-eared manuscripts, wrinkled, tired and worn out from countless journeys to other contests. (One advantage, of course, of electronic submission is that your manuscript is forever bright and new).

Incidentally, would you believe that around 10% of submissions in just about all prose contests are sent in without payment of the required reading (or entry) fees? In poetry contests, more than 50% of entries are not paid for.

And this trend has remained fairly static for the past five years. Seventeen years ago, it was virtually unheard of. But the proliferation of free contests on the internet has produced a group of hardened contestants who believe they can enter all competitions free. Needless to say, feeless entries are never read. They go straight into the recycle bin.

Of course, accidents can happen. I used to do my own preliminary sorting and in year two an unpaid entry managed to make the short list, and was even headed for a major prize, before I discovered my error. We now have a fool-proof triple-check system to ensure I don't waste my time again.

Now for the second cull. This is normally carried out by the organization's officers. Not only do they pay particular attention to the rules, they look out for unsuitable subject matter and also eliminate entries that are so poorly written as to have no chance of success. For example: *Flydough was a dog. He had four legs. Also a tail. His tail was all brown. But his head was white with brown spots. I loved Flydough. And he loved me.* Charming, yes. But that simple charm wears mighty thin over a thousand words, even in a kids' contest.

It's not until the third sorting, however, that any really serious reading takes place. (I'm speaking about *other* contests, remember, not the Tom Howard contests, where all the sorting and culling is done by Professor Konrad personally). In this third cut, entries are expertly divided into thanks-but-no-thanks and worth-further-consideration. The first category includes popular fiction (no matter how superlatively crafted) entered for a *literary* contest; artistic traditional verse submitted to a university-sponsored award; and entries in which the writing is subjectively judged to be no more than passable or even below par (except, of course, in the case of undergraduate college or university prizes and awards where originality, no matter how contrived, covers a multitude of sins).

All the worth-further-examination submissions are then either directly passed on to the final judge (or judges), or are presented to yet another intermediate panel, who select a short list of a carefully selected twenty to fifty. This list is ultimately delivered to the guest judge for his examination and final allocation of prizes and commendations. You will notice that guest judges or name judges or celebrity judges do not usually look at all the entries or even a sizable fraction of those entries. If a contest receives 1,000 entries, the guest judge would normally be expected to read no more than a carefully culled fifty. You'll be glad to hear, however, that there are always exceptions. A nationally acclaimed poet with whom I'm acquainted, insisted on reading ALL the entries for a recent contest in which she was asked to serve as a "guest judge".

Let's look at contests for popular fiction. If your manuscript makes it into the worth-further-reading stage, here are twelve points on which it will fail or succeed:

THE TITLE: Many writers often undermine a great story by a prosaic or unoriginal title. Remember, your title is the first thing a judge sees. Try to think of a title that is clever, original and relevant.

LENGTH: Many writers don't know when to stop writing. Avoid unnecessary anti-climaxes. A short story must be concise. On the other hand, it is not necessarily short. In the Tom Howard Contest your maximum limit is 5,000 words, but to sustain reader interest in a story of this precise length, your story must be strongly plotted and vividly characterized.

CUTTING: I used to say that a writer's best tool was a blue pencil. But now it is the *delete* key on your computer or typewriter. Put every word under the microscope. Is it absolutely necessary? Does your story read as well without it? Does it help make your sentences sing? Are you growing two or three words where even one would be superfluous?

FIRST LINE and FIRST PARAGRAPH: So important, because they are the first words the judge and your readers will see. Do they grab attention? Do they promise excitement, suspense, humor, intrigue?

DIALOGUE: Is it natural? Is it in character? Can you identify the speaker without the author telling you who's speaking? What functions does your dialogue perform — for instance, does it advance the plot, impart necessary background information, reveal character traits, conjure up atmosphere?

VOCABULARY: Avoid long and obscure words unless you aim to be funny or wry or ironic. While an unusual vocabulary can be an important ingredient of your ultimate or preferred style, it's not a good idea to trial it out in competitions unless you're prepared for more than your fair share of setbacks and disappointments.

ACTION: This does NOT necessarily mean violent, physical action. Your story must have a sense of movement, it must seem to be flowing rapidly towards some emotionally satisfying or terrifying or unexpected Niagara, not eddying around in circles, going nowhere. What many judges seek is fiction, carrying no overt or little violence at all, that yet comes across as a thrilling, fast-paced, suspenseful story, with a nice ironic twist at the finish.

Tied in with action are the so-called GREEK UNITIES of time, place and theme. What is your story's time span? Is it set continuously in the same place? What is its main theme? Are there any subsidiary themes? Sometimes it pays to run a story within a story. On other occasions, unnecessary sub-plots have disastrous consequences. They can undermine atmosphere and distract attention, even make your main storyline hard to follow or irrelevant.

CHARACTERIZATION is a field in which many promising writers get lost. You need to present recognizable yet offbeat, colorful yet natural, out-of-the-rut yet interesting and fascinating, seemingly real-life people. A tall order? Read widely, study the people you meet, note their little eccentricities, tricks of speech, etc.

CONFLICT is another essential ingredient. The more conflict, the better. Ideally, your characters must face and overcome conflicts with other people in your story, with themselves and with their circumstances.

THEME: Try to make the subject of your story some issue or topic that people currently consider important.

ENTERTAINMENT: Most people read stories not for enlightenment, but for pleasure. Of course, there's no reason why an author cannot provide both.

I can't speak for all other judges, but the above points detail what I look for in a short story. I can't under-emphasize the importance of that first line, that first paragraph and that first page! If your story does not grab my attention from the outset, there's no way it's going to win a prize, no matter how brilliantly it's otherwise written, no matter how breathtaking its climax, no matter how engrossing its characters. It may well make the Very Highly Commended list, but it won't win any money and it won't be published—not by me, anyway!

So now you know! Intriguing title, gripping first sentence, page-turning first page! That's the way I sort the worth-further-consideration pile. The short-listed entries are all stories that start like a rocket. And once aroused by that first paragraph, my attention is held in a vice until that satisfying last sentence on the final page.

From this initial short list, Professor Konrad and I select the actual winners by a process of reading and re-reading until finally we have a group of stories that engage our attention both emotionally and mentally. Stories that incorporate colorful characters into an engaging plot, held together with the suspenseful glue of conflict.

So what separates the big cash winners from the consolation prizes? Very little. What we look for is a story that not only offers a great read, but has something to say. Some point to make. Perhaps some social comment or an interesting philosophical interpretation or re-interpretation on matters, current or past, that still concern (or ought to concern) all of us deeply. Mind you, this sort of comment should not be laid on with a trowel. It should arise naturally, unobtrusively.

In the university story, on the other hand, a pointing finger of social concern is often all-important. Literary fiction and poetry tend to major on currently fashionable themes. At the moment, the dispossessed are receiving major attention. So are the marginalized, the psychotic and the diseased. Quirky writing styles and experimentation are also encouraged. The aim is to produce writing that is as far from the ideals of the popular short story and traditional poetry as it is possible to get. Poetry that doesn't look like poetry is especially "in". Blocks of prose and "poetic license" in the form of broken lines, disorganized spacing, lower case place names and personal pronouns coupled with a complete disregard for grammatical conventions, are especially prized.

CHAPTER TWELVE

Open Theme?

We have already discussed these magic words in previous chapters. Sometimes it is written as *No set theme* or *Theme at entrant's choice*. We have seen that the common or popular interpretation of these words does not apply to writing contests. No way! Let me list just a few of many possible qualifications:

The theme must appeal to the judge. It must be on his/her wavelength. If the judge is a lady, don't bother sending in your great story about professional wrestling or the annual re-union of Vietnam Vets.

If there is even a slight suggestion that winning entries will be considered for publication, steer well clear of Adults Only themes. Remember, all publishers like their books to be displayed and sold by book retailers far and wide. They don't like them to be hidden under the counter or lost from sight in the darkest corner of the store. They prefer them to cascade into the aisles where both children and adults can literally trip right over them.

Also steer well clear of X-rated language. Some contests will not accept even the mildest expletives, no matter how low-life the characters or excruciating their circumstances.

Some themes, as we saw in an earlier chapter, have been so flogged to death, they no longer command respect. It would be a mighty brave judge indeed who rewarded a story, poem, play or essay dealing with drug abuse. Other themes currently on the outer are accounts of college or student activities, adolescents coming to grips with peer pressure, and revenge stories of wives who get back at unfaithful or heavy-handed husbands. Also to be avoided (unless you can tell the tale from different latitudes with a different slant) are travel stories of eagerly anticipated excursions at home and abroad that went terribly wrong. And if I read any more stories about claim-jumping and gold prospecting in Alaska or Australia, I'll scream. There are other exotic places, you know. How about Canada or Mexico? Or Norway or Japan?

Political and religious subjects should also be given a wide berth, unless the contest organizers particularly state they are welcome. The Tom Howard Contests will accept poems and stories that deal forthrightly with religious and political issues—Mike Billington's *The Water Carrier* won First Prize in the tenth Tom Howard Short Story Contest— but most literary competitions will not, though few will go so far as to admit their bias. One exception is Paul Amphlett, the editor of *Peer Poetry International,* who advises with commendable forthrightness: "The submission should not be obscene, racist, boring or present ideas in the fields of Political or Religious Correctness."

Avoid being too topical. It seems an appealing idea to comment on current events while they're fresh and in the news. The problem is that by the time your story meets the judge's eye (let alone, sees print), many current headlines will be no longer be fresh, new and exciting.

Unless you're particularly clever and can ring in some brilliantly exciting transformations, don't ape a famous writer's style or subjects, or re-work stories, plays and folk tales like *Rip Van Winkle* and *The Barretts of Wimpole Street*. This is usually a recipe for failure. Don't enter a yarn about a fisherman battling a shark; or an obscure village that disappears and resurfaces every hundred years; or a budding boxer who wants to be a violinist; or a just judge who exemplifies all the virtues of small-town America; or a young lad who dreams of becoming a steamboat captain on the Mississippi. These themes have been updated, downdated, and done to death by better (and worse) writers than you.

Don't be disheartened if you don't make the charmed circle. Most likely, the judge simply had no interest in your subject matter. Less likely, but also take into account, there are a few pedants out there who carry around their own inviolable little rules about how poems or stories should be constructed. Ignore them! While clarity is certainly of the utmost importance in storytelling, how you achieve that clarity is entirely up to you.

CHAPTER THIRTEEN

Set Themes

I love competitions for stories, verse or articles on set themes, but, oddly, this is where many writers come to grief. The main reason is simply that they don't stick to the theme. The whole idea is that you should <u>focus</u> on the theme, <u>center</u> on the theme in the most original way you can imagine. But beware you don't downgrade the theme, you don't push it to one side, you don't introduce it like a casual afterthought and, above all, you don't ignore it altogether!

For me, the big advantage of the set-themed contest, is that, at one stroke, I can avoid all the pitfalls enumerated in previous chapters. I don't have to worry whether the subject matter will appeal to the judge. It doesn't really concern me overmuch who the judge is. All I have to do is think up a new wrinkle. A new approach to the subject. A different approach.

What most writers fail to remember is that a contest is exactly that. It's a *contest*! A contest between you and the rest of us. Good odds! I mean that. All you have to do is decide which paths most writers will follow and avoid those roads like the plague.

To win a contest, particularly a themed contest, your entry must be set apart from the crowd. You must think of a way to introduce or discuss the theme in a novel or arresting way. All things being equal, when the judge sees your entry, he or she must say: "This is different from the rest! Here is a fresh approach. First Prize!"

It's important to spend a fair amount of time considering various angles and options before putting pen to paper. Read up on the subject, even if you know it well, to see how other writers have tackled it in the past. And whatever the consensus is, avoid it!

Here's a good example. I won a Highly Commended award for this one. I'd have done better, if I'd known about the contest earlier and had been allowed more time to polish my prose. Even so—rough spots, errors and all—it still ended up in the top four of over seven hundred entries.

The theme was "Outback". Simply that. *Outback.* No qualifications. What would you do? Probably what almost all other submitters attempted, namely to write a story— any old story—set in the outback. But that isn't exactly what the theme is asking for. What the judge expects is not just a story set in the outback, not just backgrounded in the outback, but a tale in which *Outback* forms an intrinsic, central part. How do you make *Outback* the actual subject of the story, more important than the characters, more vital than the plot? You could personify *Outback* but that's not a good idea because you're not writing an article, you're writing a story with a great, grab-the-attention beginning, a fascinating middle and a mind-blowing finish. How about a journey to the Outback? How about a character who is seeking something tangible in the Outback, or something intangible like meaning and soul? Like the story by O. Henry where someone is seeking the soul of the city?

Three writers out of nearly seven hundred thought of this "soul" approach and we all won prizes. The other two winners saw Outback not as a vision, a nirvana, a Holy Grail, a goal or even as a possession, but as a cadence, a rhythm, an emotion. Quite a few authors attempted to re-work the old cliché about someone lost in the Outback, but that approach was doomed to failure. Avoid clichés unless you can manage to disguise them under a heavy coat of new paint.

Alongside set themes which require research and thought, are set categories in which a writer's options are likewise limited. I like these options because once again a fresh approach will almost always win, even if you're up against more polished, more experienced, more talented writers. These categories include memoirs, biographies, short documentary screenplays, articles, commentaries, parodies, critiques, and even sermons. Aside from sermons where innovations in thought are not encouraged (though presentation is), these categories offer writers golden opportunities. One, because they don't attract nearly as many entries (read *rival competitors*) as short stories and poetry, even though they usually offer the same (or better) rewards. Two, because, once again, a fresh approach will win out every time over superior polish and craftsmanship.

A few years ago, I won First Prize for a themed one-act play or short screenplay. The theme was *Addictions*. I decided to write a screenplay, rather than a stage play, because it offered greater scope. I hoped to avoid all currently press-popular addictions like drinking, smoking, gambling, drugs, etc., because every other mother's son and daughter would zero in on these "bad habits". Instead, I decided to focus on the local country club. There *are* people who are addicted to country clubs. They spend all their time there. Their whole lives revolve around the country club. If you don't believe me, read F. Scott Fitzgerald. First Prize!

The memoir category, I regard as a godsend. Your subject doesn't have to be a famous person, just an interesting or unusual person. We've all met people who'd make ideal subjects. Of course, if your subject is still alive, it's a good idea to get their approval, particularly if you intend to say anything that could be interpreted as unflattering.

I wrote a winning memoir about my own grandfather. This did present a few problems as I had to change all the names to protect my contest anonymity, but, in these circumstances, writers are usually given the opportunity to change them back before the manuscript goes to press.

(Where publication is offered, many contest organizers insist on *NO CHANGES*, but this requirement is usually waived for factual submissions like biographies and memoirs).

CHAPTER FOURTEEN

Pen Names and Other Sundries

I'm often asked why almost all contests require pen-names on entries (or no names at all) What's all this fuss about not putting your real names on entries? And what's the use of pen-names anyway? What purpose do pseudonyms serve?

Almost all writing contests and literary competitions are judged blind. In other words, the judges have no idea who their entrants are. They could well be famous writers or completely unknown authors or penpushers in between. The theory behind this stratagem is that the judges are seen as free from bias. I agree. But I don't use this system myself, because I accept the fact that I'm biased in favor of unknown and struggling writers. If the First Prize was a toss-up between a famous author and a nobody, I'd choose the soon-to-be-famous rather than the already famous every time.

Mind you, famous authors and middlingly famous authors don't usually enter prose contests. On the other hand, well-known poets frequently appear in the winning lists of poetry competitions. (The top-top echelon of poets, however, usually don't compete, because they often act as judges). There are interesting reasons behind this apparent contradiction:

A famous novelist is always well represented in your local Smiths or Borders, but you'd have to look mighty hard to find any shelving devoted to poets. A novelist in our time can become a household name, but a poet...

A best-selling novelist doesn't need the money or the prestige. Perhaps, even more importantly, he can't write short fiction anyway. It's actually far easier for an author who has mastered the craft of the short story to enter the field of novel-writing than vice versa. What's more, there are best-selling authors who actually contribute very little to the books they supposedly write. They are really public relations men who lend their names to a book that is composed collectively by a publisher's committee. I know of what I speak. I have sat on such committees myself, not as an author but as a publisher.

A publisher is first cousin to a movie producer. Both work with a strong team of assistants. Directly assisting the publisher (and often acting as a go-between with the author) are his/her chief assistant (or associate); then the editor (often confusingly called the "publisher", in which case the number one publisher is titled executive publisher or publisher-in-chief), the reader, the chief sales manager, the marketing and publicity manager, the designer, the production manager, and any number of freelance specialists and experts.

In most cases, both the editor and the reader collaborate directly with the author on the manuscript. Just how much the author actually contributes depends as much on his aggressiveness (and his clout with the executive publisher) as his literary skills.

In my case, I was contracted to write a book directly by the executive publisher. I knew him slightly because we lived in the same city and we were, of course, both members of the national publishers' association. At annual meetings, we sat at the same table. Anyway, he phoned me and explained he was in a bit of a spot because an author had unknowingly sold him a manuscript over which he no longer held any rights. The author's agent had actually sold the rights to a rival firm but had not communicated this fact to the author (which admittedly he was not obligated to do straightaway. He was only obliged to make contact with the author every six months). Anyway, this particular book was announced with much trumpeting in the trade press and when the rival publisher saw these ads, he threatened to sue. This put my publisher in a pretty fix. He had to find a substitute book fast. So he asked me if I had a suitable manuscript on hand. I didn't. But I'm the sort of person who can't bear to disappoint people. So I told him, yes, I did. Oh, joy! "What's it about?" he managed to ask, once his euphoria wore off a bit. As it happened, I'd just returned from an interview on local television. "It's set in a television station," I said quickly. "Great, John! Great! How soon can you let me have it?" Now that really put me in the hot seat. I told him I needed to polish the manuscript up a bit and suggested six weeks. We eventually settled for three.

Fortunately, I'm the sort of writer who can spin the words fast if I have to (that's the very first skill you learn when you're writing for newspapers and magazines) and I did actually put the manuscript into his eager hands within the three weeks. "What about a contract?" I asked. He was so grateful, he allowed me to write my own ticket. The only proviso he made concerned the cover. Although I could supervise the design of a cover and get it all made up, the final decision lay in the hands of the sales manager. "I'm sorry, John. I can't over-rule him. It's part of his contract. But with anybody else, you are the final court of appeal." We shook hands. Then he walked me down to the editor's office, threw the manuscript on her desk and cheerily told her, to her evident surprise, that I was in charge of the project, and that I was in fact a fellow-publisher, not just an "author" (a term of near-contempt).

When the publisher left us to get acquainted, I sat down, murmuring profuse apologies that the book had been so suddenly thrust upon her. Within thirty minutes, the frosty atmosphere had melted and we were talking away, happily exchanging caustic observations on mutual friends. The publishing world is a small world. In the end, we both agreed *Merryll Manning Is Dead Lucky* (the name of the book) was about to become an interesting experiment. "I've never worked in really close collaboration with a real publisher," she said. "And I've never worked with an editor before!" I added. [I'd always done my own editing, though I had expert assistants, including my wife whom I met in a newspaper office. She was the paper's chief proof reader. (There's a romantic story for you). This happy event occurred in those halcyon years before computers and spellchecks made life a bit harder for all of us].

Anyway, right after our pleasant chat, the editor sent the manuscript off to the in-house fiction reader with instructions that all other projects were to be dropped and that she was to give all her attention to *Merryll Manning Is Dead Lucky* immediately.

Within a few days, the reader reported back on the manuscript, and the three of us met to discuss possible changes. I turned on my charm, told the reader what a wonderful job she'd done, readily concurred to make some minor alterations and expressed myself more than happy to re-write some chapters where the writing was a little hurried and lacked polish.

A week later, we had another meeting. We all agreed the changes improved the story no end, but we still had one major sticking point. One of the chapters ended too abruptly. No trouble to flesh it out myself, I argued, although plenty of re-write people were on tap. They could indeed "refresh" the whole manuscript if that's what we wanted. I felt re-write services were not required, so that put an end to that suggestion.

After my third draft was completed, the manuscript was sent to the typesetter who at length produced initial proofs requiring correction. To my surprise, the publisher's proofing department didn't merely draw attention to all the typos, but actually made pages and pages of story and manuscript "suggestions". This action called for yet another committee meeting, this time a panel of seven: myself, the editor, the reader, a very determined lady supervisor from the proof department and her assistant, a rep from the marketing office, and a budding lawyer to point out any possible breaches of copyright or libel.

Despite strong opposition, I turned down flat almost all the panel's suggestions. I felt the manuscript read pretty excitingly as it stood. Aside from the obvious typos, I would agree to only a few minor changes. This brought a heated response from the proof lady who felt the action at the climax was not sufficiently prepared for. Once again I rejected the services of the re-write specialists, but to keep the peace, I finally agreed to pen at least one additional explanatory chapter.

Now just imagine a tyro author in that sort of set-up! Or even an experienced writer who didn't have the backing of an executive publisher! The actual book you see on sale in the bookstores could—and often does by the time the various publishing committees have completed all their combined input—finish up nothing like the author's original conception.

Well, all that seems a long digression from what purpose pseudonyms serve, but it does allow me to answer the question. Writers choose pen-names for a variety of reasons. The most usual are: (1) The writer is a publisher and therefore could well be accused of being a self-publisher (oh, horrors!); (2) the writer is already a well-known figure in (or is often identified with) some other field (like law or politics), or even some other branch of literature; (3) the writer actually craves anonymity. In my own case, I was an established publisher long before I took up writing novels (although I had contributed film reviews and movie monographs to specialized periodicals like "Films and Filming" ever since my college and university days). I was then faced with a dilemma. Why go to all the trouble of persuading another publisher to take my novels under his wing when I could do it so much better myself?

The major problem boils down to the fact that a self-publisher is not highly regarded in the book trade. Worse, self-published books, no matter how salable or superlative, are rarely reviewed. And no reviews equal no sales. So I chose as a pseudonym the name of my maternal grandfather (which happened to be my middle name anyway), Thomas Howard.

Viewpoint is another issue that vexes many writers. I usually use the first person, but have no problems with third <u>unless the whole story is told from one character's viewpoint</u>. I would then ask, why are you using impersonal third? What's the point? Why not make the story more involving by using first person? I hope you can come up with a good argument. As it happens, in my case, I can. If you read my story, "Mexican Autumn", you'll see that it could easily be re-worked from the doctor's point of view. My problem is I'm not a native Mexican. I don't really know how Mexicans think. I, the author, am an observer, not a protagonist.

Frankly, I'm a firm believer that mystery or detective stories should be written in the first person, in order to play fair with the reader. But otherwise your choice of a narrative point of view depends on what you think is the best way to tell the story with maximum impact.

I'm often asked at writers' conferences and so-called "manuscript clinics", how many characters are the ideal for a short story? The conventional wisdom holds that you need only as many characters as the story demands. This doesn't tell us much. But obviously one hundred characters is far too many for a short story, and fifty would seem equally absurd. You might get away with twenty in a long story. But I believe your aim should be to use a minimum number, in order to concentrate the reader's interest and attention. For example, in the short story, "Ash", which won first prize in Tom Howard Contest Nine, author Peter Job used only four characters, despite the fact that his story stretched to nearly 8,000 words. And of those four characters, one didn't enter until the story was in its final phase!

CHAPTER FIFTEEN

How to Find Suitable Contests

If you're a poet, look no further than Winning Writers. The site address is http://www.winningwriters.com

Why do I recommend Winning Writers? Simple! I know the editor personally. I know he makes a scrupulous effort not only to eliminate all scam contests, but to expose them. And although some free, and some very modest contests are listed, I stand by all of them.

Finding suitable prose contests, can be a little more difficult. The Open Directory used to be a fine place for up-to-date contest listings, but this is no longer the case. I therefore recommend Google as the premier medium for "prose contests".

In the previous edition of this book, I gave the advice: "Don't try to win the Pulitzer first up. Try your hand, get some experience with the smaller contests, then work up the ladder." I'd like to change this. Back then, few contests published their short lists. What are short lists? Their size and nature varies a little from contest to contest. In contests with a guest judge who reads only selected entries, the short list comprises those twenty to fifty entries from which the guest judge makes a final selection.

In most contests, however, entries are initially divided into a "long list", which comprises all those submissions thought worthy of further consideration. By close reading and other processes, this is ultimately shortened to a "short list." Unfortunately, most competitions keep details of their short lists a secret, so contestants are left in the dark as to whether their entries at least made it through to the final selection committees. At present, however, both the Tom Howard and Margaret Reid Contests are actually placing all the short listed details on their website pages of Results, so now you can find out whether your poem or story was considered worthy of a closer and more exacting scrutiny for a cash prize or commended award.

Admittedly, it's most disappointing to discover that all that $5,350 in beautiful cash has slipped through your fingers. But you now have some tangible encouragement. Your poem or story could well win a prize in a smaller contest where it was not up against such stiff competition.

It's also possible that your entry could be made more attractive with a little more polish. The margin that separates a cash-winning entry from the commended or short-listed, is often extremely small. And there's usually nothing to stop you re-entering your revised entry in next year's contest!

So my present advice to "test the waters" by submitting your story or poem to a large contest first up. Why not? You could be another Dan Brown or Agatha Christie, or Robert Frost or Agnes Duer Miller.

CHAPTER SIXTEEN

Frequently Asked Answers

1. "Open theme" does not mean anything goes. Phrases like "unrestricted subject matter" and "themes at competitors' choice" do not mean all subjects will be considered. If publication is offered, for example, it is absolutely obligatory that contestants limit themselves to subjects suitable for publication. If a contest is sponsored by a conservative writing group, it is assumed entrants will have enough sense to tailor their subject matter accordingly.

2. Word limits usually mean exactly that. Not generally that. The idea that a 5% or 10% leeway may be allowable is often false. Some contests, and most particularly flash fiction competitions (that is contests that impose a limit of two thousand words or less), will disqualify entries that are even one word over the limit. Before software programs did their work for us, entries had to be counted by hand. A hyphenated word was usually regarded as a single, unless the hyphens extended over more than two words. Thus "by-pass" was counted as one word, "four-in-hand" as three. An abbreviation (e.g. "Mrs") or an acronym (e.g. "N.A.T.O.) were also generally regarded as one word. The story's title (and sub-title, if any) was not usually counted. However, these were not rules. They were generalizations. Different software programs count problem words such as the above in different ways. To counter this, some flash fiction contests with a low but strictly enforced limit – say 500 words –

will specify say, 1,800 characters, instead. But in some cases, you are still not sure if they count the heading or your contestant pen-name, identification number, etc. So it's always a good idea to aim for at least ten or twenty or maybe even thirty words less than the allowable maximum.

3. Entry forms are filed alphabetically, but not the entries themselves. Once an entry goes into the contest pile, it's effectively lost for the duration of the contest and cannot be retrieved to make changes and alterations. Entries can often be withdrawn completely, but reading fees will not be refunded because your submissions have already gone through the judging process. If you are unhappy with your entry and wish to send in an up-dated version, do so. You will usually need to fill in a fresh entry form (if such forms are required) and pay the entry fee again. [But, as said before, we writers are not by nature terribly good judges of our own work. Publishing an anthology of prizewinning entries brings me into direct contact with authors who want to make changes. Even major prize holders are often not content. They send back the proofs with copious alterations on every page. In not one single case have I accepted these changes (unless, of course, there was a typo on the original manuscript). Some contests will not allow re-writes on principle. But I've never accepted them for the simple reason that the earlier version was the one that gained my approval. If I wasn't absolutely delighted, thrilled and enthralled—if I'd thought the story could have been improved in any way—I would never have awarded it a prize in the first place].

4. "Rhyming poetry" in contest lingo almost always means traditional verse. I and many other poets see

no reason why free verse should be exclusively non-rhyming. Or, to put our proposition another way, why can't free verse use rhymes? If you exclude rhymes, the verse is hardly "free", is it? As far as contest organizers are concerned, however, if you employ rhymes, you risk having your entries classified or re-classified as traditional verse and judged accordingly. One adjudicator even advised me that I should join a poetry group so that I could learn the basic rules of scanning and "proper meter," and thus be in a position to apply these rules to my free verse!

5. There is no way in the world that an entry without an entry fee (where called for) will be read by anyone. Unpaid submissions are culled by clerical staff and never reach the judges.

6. I usually avoid contests that insist on elaborate technical presentation requirements. Some well-regarded contests not only spell out an approved page set-up including margins, fonts and points, but also enforce obligatory methods of binding. Others call for detailed information on cover sheets and/or index cards and some even specify how to address return envelopes. Fiddling with all these ridiculous rules not only wastes an inordinate amount of creative time, but just one slip-up could result in instant disqualification.

7. Most of the world's prestigious contests, awards, prizes, etc., are wary of the electronic revolution and insist on carrying on exclusively with hard copy, snail mail, and traditional print. Some contests, however, do accept submissions in both hard copy and electronically via email or by uploading the file or by pasting the copy in a box at the contest website. Contests which accept entries exclusively by electronic means are (with five or six

notable exceptions) not highly regarded in the literary community (although many are perfectly legitimate).

8. Pen-names are almost always obligatory in literary competitions. The feeling is that they tend to keep the identity of contributors a secret from the judges. This is true enough. But what's the point? Why bother? "Name" writers always steer well clear of competitions for fear their contributions might receive the ratings they truly deserve, like "Commended" or "Highly Commended". So what the judges would see, if real names were used, are names that mean little, signify less, and are no more informative than a phone book. When choosing a pen-name, however, be careful. If your story is told in the first person always select a pen-name of unmistakably the same gender. Nothing irritates a judge more than to read the first page of a story and then discover the narrator is a man not a woman, or vice versa. An irritated judge will stay irritated and never re-read your submission in a kindly light. Never!

9. Four tips for a winning entry (poem, short story or essay): (a) Think of a catchy but suitable title. (b) Spend a lot of time on your opening lines. Make them so interesting the reader can't wait to read on! (c) Keep up the pace throughout. Eliminate any slow passages. Hurtle like an express train towards a logical and satisfying conclusion. (d) Try to be different. Take risks! Ask yourself: What will other entrants write about? How will they tackle the subject?

10. Avoid contests in which the same groups of writers appear in the winning lists, time after time, year after year. These usually turn out to be smalltime events, sponsored by regional writing groups. The

judge is often drawn from the group's own ranks or from close connections. Naturally, although the entries are disguised with pseudonyms, the judge will tend to favor works that he can easily recognize. To avoid this problem, some contests will not accept entries from previous prize-winners. I don't impose any such rules, because I find that most writers find it difficult to repeat a previous success. I often rate their subsequent efforts as disappointing in that they fail to measure up to the high standards previously achieved.

11. If you wish to succeed in contests, don't bother with courses that develop "speed writing". These courses aim to help you write as fast as you speak. But the way you speak is often a far cry from the polish and craftsmanship needed to tell an exciting and involving story. Even a practiced professional will need to spend time polishing and refining that story if it is to have a fair chance of winning a contest or actually being published for money. As to how much time I personally spend on a story, it depends partly on the length, partly on any problems encountered during the actual writing. In order to overcome "writer's block", I actually work on three or four things at the same time. Say a film review (or a book review or a press release or editorial), and a magazine article, and a novel or a short story, or a poem. If I run into a snag, I put that piece aside for a few days. But let's say everything is running smoothly—and I'm writing a short story. My aim is to write about 500 words a day. I constantly revise what I've written, trying to choose the best possible words to express my meaning, and trying to keep my sentences as short as possible, and yet also introduce some variety and snappy synonyms and images into the text. At the end of five days, if all

goes well, I should complete 2,500 words. I then spend a final day or two on revision. Then I put the story aside for as long as possible, — a month would be ideal. When I take up the manuscript again, I look at the story from the viewpoint of a reader. If anything is not clear, I add explanatory material. If there are any slow passages, I eliminate or condense them.

12. It's okay to have multiple points of view in a novel, but in a short story always be consistent. Never change viewpoints. If you start off in the first person, keep it that way! Also, treat flashbacks with caution. It requires a great deal of skill to use a flashback effectively in a short story. Remember, a flashback is a break in the narrative. It is a break which, in all but the most skilful hands, can dissolve the reader's attention. If you must provide background information, do so in the body of the story through dialogue. (Or use a first person viewpoint in which previous events can be subtly detailed through your character's thoughts and reactions).

13. As a general rule, the earlier you submit to a contest, the greater your chances of success. And don't be afraid to send in multiple entries where this is allowed. However, unless you receive a discount on your entry fees, it is more prudent to send in entries one at a time as you complete them, rather than send them in all at once. It's hard enough competing with other entrants, let alone competing with yourself.

14. Oddly, while traditional writing rules are important in stories and poems because they help to hold the reader's attention, in essays they are generally of less account. My favorite essayist is Jerome K. Jerome. Part of his charm is that he wanders all over

the place and pays no regard to "rules". (His short stories, on the other hand, are extremely well-constructed. *The Fawn Gloves*, one of his most famous stories, is told in flashback. The reader's attention is piqued by the very opening paragraph: "Always he remembered her as he saw her first: the little spiritual face, the little brown shoes pointed downwards, their toes just touching the ground; the little fawn gloves folded upon her lap." Notice the astute use of punctuation and repetition to heighten tension. A master like Jerome doesn't slavishly obey the rules. He makes the rules serve his purpose).

15. Speaking of essays, polish is always super-important. I once conducted an essay contest for writers on a writers' web site. To my amazement, at least eighty per cent of entries were poorly written. The feeling seemed to be, *Look, I'm writing a piece for writers on how I achieved my first sale. Writers are only interested in facts. Style doesn't matter.* Believe me, style always matters, whether it's a letter to the editor, a filler, a factual article, or even a piece for a special interest group. One stylistic problem that most entrants were probably unaware of, let alone made any attempts to overcome, revolved around a potential overuse of the personal pronoun. Here's a typical opening paragraph: *I achieved my first sale in 1954. Back then, I was working as a stable boy for Hot-iron Harry, the horse trainer. I'd spent years as an apprentice but I didn't succeed. I grew too tall. So now I was reduced to tending stables. I decided to write how wages were poor and working conditions were bad in the racing industry. I wanted to send my piece to* The New York Times, *but then I decided that maybe I was over-reaching myself. So I thought I'd*

send my news to the editor of The Podunk Press *instead. Imagine my surprise and joy! The editor printed my item. And I received two dollars too. But I had forgotten about Harry. Harry was mad as a meat-ax. I told him I was grown up now. I didn't have to ask Hot-iron Harry if I wanted to write a news item. I was my own boss. And I sent my news to* The Podunk, *because I wanted to see it printed.*

16. Another thing I hate is an over-use of the verb "to be", particularly the past participle. A typical sample: *Sam was always like a brother to me. He was not a real brother of course. He was just a friend. But he was always a real friend when I needed him most. My family was not real well-off. My dad was a butcher by trade but most folk in Cowpatch County were fusspot vegetarians. They were farmers, not ranchers or cattlemen. They were used to eating their own produce and trading among themselves. Their mayor was a man named Scrivener Scopes. Mr Scopes was a large man, grown fat with daily tithes of potatoes, leeks, eggs and home-made custards. Although he was inclined to be friendly with his friends, he was dogmatic to a tee with a man like my father. Although he was well-used to Scopes' ribbing and insults, dad was unhappy that he was continually used as the town's standing joke. In fact, he was just about to give the whole meat trade away, when he was accosted by a stranger who was anxious to buy a whole mess of sausages. Dad was naturally beside himself with glee, but also he was very surprised. Why was the stranger buying so many sausages? Was he a dog-lover? Was he treating a bus-load of school-kids? Or was he just plain nuts?*

17. Next to a dull, humdrum title, an unexciting first paragraph and an unsatisfying finish, the biggest

killer of potentially prizewinning short stories is flat writing. I mean writing that has no color, no style, no pizzazz. Sentence follows sentence—subject, verb, object; subject, verb, predicate—with all the monotony of a didgeridoo. Thinking of a way out of this routine should be a writer's first priority. How about short sentences? Then you might try a few much longer sentence constructions, interleaved with a few colorful similes and metaphors. You might even ask a question or two. And provide snappy answers.

18. As in everything else, practice makes perfect. Looking at the samples of allegedly "bad" writing I composed above, you must admit that despite their faults, they actually read quite entertainingly. I tried to make my writing as flat and off-putting as possible, but I couldn't manage to do it!

CHAPTER SEVENTEEN

Ten Sure-Fire Rejection Stratagems

1. Don't bother to read any of the Contest's previous prize-winning entries.
2. Ignore the Contest's requirements, particularly relating to length and entry fees.
3. Pay no regard to those stupid old fuddy-duddy rules about punctuation and spelling.
4. If writing in the first person, make sure the judge knows it by using the pronoun "I" as often as possible. Or worse still, draw attention to the fact in a poem by the consistent use of a lower case "i".
5. Keep your writing flat as a board. Ensure it has no tone or color. If composing a poem, forget about imagery altogether.
6. Use at least one cliché in every line or sentence. Make sure in rhyming poetry that God's love is always found in heaven above, and that the moon always shines best in June
7. Avoid originality at all costs.
8. Endeavor to spread your opening paragraph or stanza over the entire first page.
9. Consistently employ one inverted comma (') for dialogue instead of two (").
10. Always send a rough draft of your work, never a polished, thoroughly checked manuscript.

CHAPTER EIGHTEEN

Ten Quick Ways To Catch the Judge's Eye

1. A professionally presented manuscript.
2. Unusual, intriguing title.
3. Powerful, attention-grabbing, opening line.
4. Flexible writing style.
5. Interesting setting.
6. Colorful imagery or characters.
7. Clever metaphors or snappy dialogue.
8. Entrancing language or page-turning narrative.
9. A breath-taking, but logical finish.
10. Originality.

CHAPTER NINETEEN

Maximizing Poetry

In Chapter Eleven, I detailed Twelve Points which would determine if an entry in a contest for popular fiction ultimately reached the Chief Judge's desk, or if that entry was destined to fall by the wayside. Some of these considerations obviously apply to poetry competitions as well, but, unless you're submitting a long narrative poem or a verse play, dialogue, characterization and an observance of the so-called Greek unities, do not usually apply. But other factors do. So, at the risk of repeating some of my advice, here are seven points that are especially applicable to verse:

THE TITLE: The first thing the judge sees, particularly in large contests where the chief judge is emailed a long list of titles, some of which will ignite his or her enthusiasm and which he/she will read first. I have just finished re-editing the first Tom Howard anthology, *End of Season*, and I was struck by the enormous vitality and poetic quality of all 35 of the poems chosen for publication. The title of the winning poem was "Fritillary". Now that is certainly an unusual title, absolutely guaranteed to catch the judge's eye. The third prize went, appropriately enough, to "Jeremy Johnson Jackson the Third". Another unique title! Second prize was won by the more prosaic, "Train Journey", but that title captured my attention too, because when you read some of my books like "Merryll Mannning on the Rim of Heaven", you'll soon realize I'm a railroad buff. (It always pays to read a few of the judge's books or at least find out a few things about them). Titles that stand out among the Highly Commended entries include "South west down under", "following", "Dawn at the Cross", "End of Season", "Nothing", "Over the Road, Down by the Creek", "Mackay", and "Hindsight 20/20".

THEME: A successful poem must have a consistent theme. You can't start off writing about the bridges at Toko-Ri and suddenly switch to the apple tree in your neighbor's garden unless you make some sort of connection. It goes without saying that the theme must interest the judge. The greatest poem ever written about Swan Lake will head straight for the reject bin if the judge is tone deaf. This why it's so important not only to find out as much as you can about the judge but to enter not just one poem but five or six.

FIRST LINE AND FIRST STANZA: The first words the judge will read after the title. If he's not impressed, most likely he'll only glance at the body of your entry.

IMAGERY AND VOCABULARY: Poetic license allows the poet to use unusual words and juxtapositions to create unusual, figurative images. Few poets avail themselves of this freedom. They stick to the commonplace. Yet in verse you are free to use your imagination. Here, for instance, are the first two lines of "Dawn at the Cross" by Jonathan Elsom: "Like spritely aproned waiters / Ibis stalk." Here is the opening stanza from my "Art Gallery to Quay: A Boy Fifteen in '53" which was commended in several national contests. (Don't be wary of long titles. You don't have to pay for them): "It's a long soulless walk from Art Gallery / to Circular Quay. / The paths are petite-colonnaded. / The night watchman has a key." I have tried not to be too obtuse, but I'm sure you can all compose far more effective images with more powerful and unique juxtapositions.

CADENCE AND RHYTHM: Cadence depends on devices like alliteration and assonance, as well as rhyme. Rhythm depends not only on meter, but on the natural swish and swing of words and phrases. Even free verse must have rhythm – an informal rhythm, an inconsistent rhythm, but a beat, a musical beat nonetheless.

RESONANCE: Your poem must sound as good as it looks. Remember that all poetry is principally designed to be read aloud, to be recited. Many poems which seem to possess all the qualities of prize-winning verse on the printed page, often fail the recitation test.

ARTISTRY AND ENTERTAINMENT: Some so-called "serious" poets conveniently ignore the fact that poetry, like all artistic endeavors, has a purpose. That purpose is usually to entertain, to enhance, to uplift, to spread joy. A didactic poem can have a serious purpose certainly, but the aim is still, in my view, to communicate. I am not in favor of poetry in which the author locks himself in a literary vault and refuses to communicate with his or her readers.

APPENDIX ONE

FIRST PRIZE

Southern Cross Literary Competition 2002

"Fan-Fan"

An Essay by John Howard Reid

Fan-Fan is a rabbit. A pure white rabbit except for her red, luminous eyes and a pink lining inside each of her ears. She lives with me in villa one at number forty-eight Sunshine Crescent, Woodbury. Not that she is particularly aware of her surroundings. To her, home is five comparatively small rooms, — hallway, laundry, TV room, bedroom one and bedroom two. She never ventures into the kitchen, bathroom or toilet and is not allowed in the computer alcove. Only rarely will I treat her to a little run around my small backyard. In fact, she has to be coaxed to go outside. But once running free on the grass, she needs to be bribed with a carrot to come back in or be frightened by my sudden disappearance.

I love Fan-Fan and wouldn't willingly cause her any pain or distress, so the backyard playground is rarely used. At least I know why she panics, if I don't stand guard. She smells cats.

But why Fan-Fan will never enter the kitchen, bathroom or toilet is a complete mystery. Not that I'm complaining. It's nice to have a couple of rooms rabbit-free, completely to myself.

Fan-Fan is not stupid. She knows she's not allowed in the computer section. She also knows why. She eats electric wires. Bites them right through. I can't understand why she hasn't electrocuted herself. Truly a rabbit with forty-nine lives.

Of course, being a rabbit, she often can't resist coming into the forbidden zone, if she realizes I'm busy elsewhere. She knows she's disobedient. She knows she's deliberately doing wrong. I've only to say, "Fan-Fan!" in a reasonably cross voice, and she will hop away so fast she pretends to herself that no sin was committed. You can almost see the halo over her head as she stretches herself out on the bedroom carpet and looks up at me as if to say, "That wasn't me you saw just now in the computer alcove. That must have been some other white rabbit."

Fan-Fan is a fussy eater. She knows what she likes. Carrots, crispwheat biscuits, cardboard boxes. For a real treat, fresh broccoli. If really hungry, she'll tolerate pet-shop meals of rabbit and guinea pig mixtures and pellets. Occasionally, she'll eat a tomato or even an apple. She never seems to drink much water. Presumably she extracts all the juice she needs from the quarter-pound of carrots she munches through daily. At least she has no trouble finding her way to my bedroom in the daytime.

Yes, she does have a little home of her own — an old but capacious cage (the word "cage" is a misnomer as the door is always permanently jammed open) in the laundry where she eats all her meals and deposits all her doings on old newspapers. Fan-Fan and I have found a tip-top use for *The Woodbury Clarion-Gazette* and its rival *The Woodbury Wordsmith-Bugle*. I challenge anyone to come up with a more meaningful way of expressing displeasure with editorial and advertising content.

A firm believer in the old adage that cleanliness is next to godliness, Fan-Fan will often spend hours at her toilette, brushing her fur and enthusiastically licking it into shape. Unfortunately, her timing is not the best. The incredible volume of noise emitted in this operation colors my dreams, carrying me back to a Ziegfeld Follies tonsorial parlor featuring a fleet of comic barbers sharpening razors on lengthy leather strops.

Fan-Fan's teeth are a bit of a problem. Being a rodent, she's equipped with incisors that require constant gnawing to keep in trim. Early on, she found that books met this requirement more than adequately, provided they were solidly bound. Her favorite proved to be one of my own. The spine seemed exactly right. She could get her teeth right into it. Having gnawed the spines from all my author's copies, she then started on the collected works of Sir Walter Scott. "Enough is enough!" I cried. Unthinkable that Ivanhoe, Rob Roy and Quentin Durward should meet the same fate as my own less immortal gifts to the world! At this point I hit upon a stout box, — a cardboard box packed with receipts, invoices, bank statements, shopping dockets and check butts. All the dreary junk that so delights actuaries, accountants, auditors and IRS men. Fan-Fan was overjoyed. You should see her, head tilted to one side, eyes closed in ecstasy as she rips into this trash, shredding it into digestible, mouth-watering pieces.

Fan-Fan will tolerate petting but she hates to be picked up. Understandable. Human beings look like the Colossus of Rhodes to a little, ground-hugging rabbit.

When I first acquired Fan-Fan (the best ten dollars I've ever spent), she'd often give me a friendly little nip by way of telling me that she liked me. I had to demonstrate to her very plainly that her friendly little nips were often quite painful. Her "Daddy" did not have thick, furry skin. I danced around the room, holding my nipped finger, crying, sobbing and carrying on a treat. She got the message. Now when I pat her fur, she turns her little head and buries her cheek in my hand. This is her alternative way of showing affection.

Unlike all my previous pets, — cats, dogs, mice, guinea pigs, birds, — rabbits do not talk. Not generally anyway. If you tread on her paw, she will utter a rumbling, throaty growl. Otherwise, she says nothing. She communicates solely by mime. And very cleverly too. Hungry, she will run into her cage, circle her near-empty bowl (she has eaten all the edible components of the mixture) and dash back to me. She repeats this maneuver until I finally get the message. Desirous of going downstairs — she dislikes hopping down the stairs by herself in the dark (though she will make the effort in an emergency) — she sits like a porcelain statue at the entrance to the kitchen, waiting for me to ask, "Like to go downstairs, Fan-Fan?" Whereupon, she'll bounce to the top of the stairwell, wait for me to turn on the light and find my slippers. It's fatal to enquire, "Carrot, Fan-Fan?" Her answer is to jump into the air, twisting and turning, and then dash madly around the room. Take that as an enthusiastic yes.

Although she knows perfectly well that her name is Fan-Fan, she will not necessarily emerge from her favorite hiding places when I call. This is her way of demonstrating her individuality and asserting her independence. If she is really angry about something — she loves to be coaxed to do things like moving out of the way when I'm sweeping the carpet and won't tolerate simply being ignominiously picked up and put down — she goes on strike, refusing to eat, or leave the laundry, until I make amends. A particularly sweet-smelling, crispy carrot will usually do the trick.

I'm not sure Fan-Fan knows she's a rabbit, though she can do all the marvelous things rabbits do, such as continuously twitching her nose and twisting her ears simultaneously in crazily different directions like a pair of radar antennae. Sometimes, she thinks she's a statue. Other times, a miniature Marcel Marceau. Two clues to her lack of identity: — She can't stand Bugs Bunny and is indifferent to her reflection in a mirror.

Fan-Fan is not only a companion but my friend. She'll often lie patiently at my feet for hours while I'm working. Never once has she scolded me for being late with her dinner or leaving her alone all day to guard the house. The only things she resents — being picked up, or roused on for accidents she couldn't help — are affronts to her dignity.

Although she recognizes only five words of English, Fan-Fan has excellent powers of deduction. She responds to the tones of my voice and applies them to present circumstances. No use upbraiding her for something she did yesterday. She has no conception of past or future. She lives entirely in present continuous.

Her five words? *Carrot, downstairs, Fan-Fan, good-girl* and *ah-ah!* The last does not express surprise but displeasure. Tell Fan-Fan *ah-ha!* and she'll cease her mischief and put her head right down on the floor. "I'm sorry. I couldn't help it. I'm only a rabbit after all."

Why call her Fan-Fan? Thereby hangs a tale. My childhood hero wasn't Errol Flynn's sturdy Robin Hood or Robert Taylor's gallant Ivanhoe or Tyrone Power's dashing Zorro or even Gene Kelly's dancing D'Artagnan, but Gerard Philippe as a stylish *Fan Fan La Tulipe*. But I usually tell visitors the name derives from her stubby little tail which resembles the stem of a closed fan. There are few Gerard Philippe fans in Woodbury.

Of course, her name is a mistake. I thought she was a boy. Too late, I discovered my error. Rabbits don't take to name-changes in mid-life, so she and I are stuck with it. Fortunately, she will never know.

Life is so simple for a little white rabbit.

APPENDIX TWO

HIGHLY COMMENDED

Scribblers Literary Contest 2002

Jo's Heaven

A Short Story by John Howard Reid

My name is Micaela Morris. I need to confess all I know about Jo's Heaven.

I'd always wanted to go to Jo's Heaven. Ever since I was a kid, back at Hedley's Creek. Every day, walking home from school, I'd pass the turn-off — a narrow, sandy track, scarcely wide enough for a single car. I used to dream of that old signpost, leaning back at a crazy angle, pointing to the sky: *Jo's Heaven, 117.*

Finally, I plucked up enough courage to ask mum, "Ever been to Jo's Heaven? What's it like?"

"No, I never. And I never been curious about it neither, young lady. One hundred and seventeen miles of nothing.

Just mulga. Who'd ever want to go to Jo's Heaven? Not me, that's for sure."

"Why's it called Jo's Heaven?"

"Who knows? Who cares? I got no time for your silly questions, Micah. Dad will be home any minute now, wanting his dinner. If you've got no homework, you can help me here in the kitchen."

Dad took me to school in his truck every morning on his way to work at the timber mill. But every afternoon when I walked home, I stopped at that crazy signpost and craned my eyes down that sandy track which ran straight as a grayish ribbon through the mulga scrub to the horizon.

One afternoon, I had a surprise. Someone was using the track. It doesn't rain much in Hedley's Creek. But after that morning's downpour, I saw fresh tire marks in the wet sand. I even followed them for about a mile down the road, just to make sure there wasn't a nearby house or farm, hiding in the mulga. I'd never heard of anyone living on the road to Jo's Heaven, but it was just possible.

I kept dreaming about Jo's Heaven. I imagined all sorts of romantic variations from magic kingdoms and ensorcelled fiefdoms, to luxuriant valleys brimming with wildlife, to stony deserts cold and bare as a hermit's heart.

Finally I realized my dream. I was eighteen years old, and had a good job at Fraser's Family Store, which enabled me to pay off a little car of my own. I told mum and dad I intended to stay overnight with my friend, Kate Fraser — which was true. She'd offered to accompany me, but at the last moment, she chickened out. When I turned my little Datsun Bluebird down the path to Jo's Heaven early that Saturday afternoon, I was alone.

About thirty miles down the track, I stopped the engine. I couldn't pull over to the side of the road. No room! Lord knows what I'd do if another car came along. I suppose one of us would have to back up to a natural clearing where the stones and boulders were less prolific and the scrub at its thinnest. Anyway, I stopped and listened. You didn't pick up much over the noise of the engine, but now I could hear a couple of crows cawing over a dead fox or some other little animal. I could also make out the steady hum of insects and the gentle sound of the wind stirring dust and leaves. All the usual music of the bush country, but here the notes seemed underpinned or overlaid by something else. The scrub itself seemed to radiate a high-pitched melody of its own, — a sound made visible in the heat-haze that hung over the near horizon, a sound you could almost touch in the flickering shadows and sparks of light that gleamed from stones and shiny pebbles in the gray-sandy soil.

Ten miles further on, the road dipped and then rose sharply up a steep hill. Ever had the feeling you were driving right into the sky? That was it. You expected to catch a marvelous view from the crest, but my hopes were dashed. An identical mulga scrub spread out before me in exactly the same monotonous pattern I'd left behind. Only the sky with its wispy bank of ski-tracked clouds presented any visual challenge.

The road never veered to the right or the left. At times, thin, gnarled branches brushed up against the car, trying to stop its progress. I ploughed on regardless, keeping careful watch on the mileage indicator. Perhaps there was nothing at the end of the road. No settlement, no houses, not a sign of civilization at all. I might drive right through Jo's Heaven without knowing it and end up in the desert.

116! The mulga showed no sign of thinning out, the track itself no sign of coming to an end. Another half-mile clicked by, and no change. Wait! A strange twinkling and flashing of light ahead. And the track was definitely curving to the right. Relief at last in this road that had no turning.

Rounding the bend, I almost ran straight into the back of a battered old pick-up truck, parked in front of a tumbledown shanty, built of hessian and wooden crates.

And here the road really did come to an abrupt halt. No turning circle. It was stopped short by a ridge of stone and sand — no more than ten or twelve feet high — that seemed to run right around the basin.

Resisting the impulse to climb the hill straightaway, I walked up to the shack that sheltered in the hollow between ridge and road. It was a job to find the entrance. Turned out to be no more than a hessian curtain in the back "wall", but I pulled it aside and shouted, "Anyone home!" Just to be on the safe side. There seemed no windows in the shack and I didn't waste further time trying to see through the gloom. Anyone for miles around would have heard my car coming and noticed the clouds of dust it was stirring up along the track.

So this dead-end was Jo's Heaven. What a disappointment, after all those dreams! All those romantic fancies had come down to an abandoned truck and a stinking shack. Yes, it did smell – to high heaven all right.

Driving all those miles through endless scrub for nothing.

I'd climb the ridge anyway and take a photo to prove I was here. A timely reminder to forget any tempting fancies in the future.

Wrong again! At the top of the ridge, Jo's Heaven spread out in an endless field of multi-colored stars. Clear to the horizon, the gibber desert, thickly mantled with wind-polished stones and pebbles, shone in a dazzling array of light – mostly flecks of bright red with occasional layers of reddish browns and purples. No trees or shrubs, no grass. The only relief from its thousands of twinkling mirrors, a series of irregular light red or dark gray hollows where the wind had scooped out all the quartz pebbles and translucent stones, exposing the desert's red dust.

Picking up some of the pebbles, I let them roll against my hand, watching them flash red, brown and blue as they caught the sun. Then I threw them in the air, marveling as they gathered up companions, all glinting like so many multi-colored marbles as they tumbled down the ridge.

"Is someone there? Someone there!"

The cry came from behind a small boulder on the desert floor. Clambering down on the slippery stones, I just managed to avoid a few nasty falls before I found the old man. A bundle of torn and dirty rags, sheltering in the shade.

"A king brown got me," he said.

"King brown? A mulga snake?"

"Early this morning. Right leg. Just above the ankle."

I looked down. Below the worn cuffs of his trousers, the leg was an ugly red, swollen to almost twice normal size.

"Leave me be! Don't touch it! Hurts like hell, but there's nothing you can do. I don't want to die alone. Thank God! Thank God!"

"I've got a car. I can take you back to Hedley's Creek."

"Don't be stupid, girlie. Can't move. Couldn't even make it to the top of the ridge. Get me some water. From the shack. Don't want to die of thirst. You'll find a jug on the shelf. Fill it from the tap. Tank water. But don't drink it yourself. Should be boiled. Doesn't matter no more, – for me."

"I've got water in the car."

"Just fill up the jug, – it'll do me all right."

"You're sure you want to stay here?" I asked.

"Can't move, I told you. I'd like to get up. But I can't. I don't want to die. But I will. Even if you got me to Hedley's Creek, there's not a thing anyone could do. Not a thing in heaven or hell. No anti-venom against the king brown. That's why he's king. Just stay with me 'til it's time. Won't be long. Maybe I'll see the stars come out. For the last time. That's a sight to see, girlie. A sight to see. And promise me one thing. Just leave me here when I go.

Don't try to bury me. Don't gather up any stones. I don't want a marker. Nothing. The gibber looks after its own. The foxes and the dingoes and the crows can have me, – and I'll be part of the desert. I'll be one with the gibber at last. But don't leave 'til I go. Funny thing. Lived alone, you know that? But I don't want to die alone. Promise!"

I nodded my head.

"Promise!" His eyes were glazed.

"I promise."

A deep sigh pulled his lips apart. "One good thing anyhow, girlie. No more making that two thirty-four mile round trip to Hedley's Creek. A big deal once a month. For supplies. Can't grow a twig in the gibber. Nor the mulga, – just dust and scrub."

"Is the gibber always like this? Thousands of colored stars?"

"Yeah. But sundown, – that's the real glory time, girlie. That's how the place got its name, you know that? It's heaven upside down."

"Are you, Jo?"

"No. No way! The name's Dave Gould. Used to work for a scientist bloke. A long time ago, girlie. A long time ago. Took part in the first atomic test, you know that? I know this country. Every waterhole. Every tree. Every shrub. Every blind inch of this desert. I know it all."

"Why's it called Jo's Heaven? Who's Jo?"

"I haven't the faintest, girlie. Not the faintest. Maybe the real Jo never saw this place. Maybe some old prospector called it Jo, after his favorite wife, – or daughter. Or just some girl he knew. Or maybe he just couldn't spell. What does it matter? Only the wind knows for sure. But Jo's Heaven is like most other places, girlie, – it's heaven or hell, just the way you make it yourself. Glory or damnation, the gibber don't care one way or the other. Not one damn way or the other."

"How long have you been here, Dave?"

"Ten years. Twelve. A man loses count of time in Jo's Heaven. Only months matter. When his supplies run out."

"No electricity. No water. Tank almost empty. Just sludge. How did you manage all these years?" I asked. "Don't you have a family? A pension?"

No answer.

"Dave!"

I nerved myself to touch his forehead. You could feel the heat rushing out of him. His eyes were closed, his lips drawn back. He was dead.

I waited for the dying sun to light up the gibber like a fairyland, an enormous pontoon of party lights stretching at least ten or maybe twenty miles to the horizon. As the first stars hit the sky, I kept my promise.

True to my word, I've remained silent all these years.

Leaving everything as it was, I turned my car around at twilight and just headed back to Hedley's Creek. In the distance, I could hear a pack of dingoes howling. Somewhere close by, a snake, a king brown – the serpent of Jo's Heaven – stirred himself from the rabbit or goanna burrow in which he'd sheltered throughout the day.

And now the king was truly king.

He ruled Jo's Heaven alone.

APPENDIX THREE

THIRD PRIZE, SUN CITY POETRY AWARDS 2003

The Actor Deprived of His Voice

A Post-Operative Soliloquy

For Jack Hawkins

"Good morning, Jack!"
But my mirror mimes empty words.
Singing swords not just blunted
or incomplete, but violently absent.
My mouth a mere mummer's show,
now delighting in darkness,

that mummifies the Bard's meters,
whispering not the merest scant of breath,
not even a chant of inarticulate moans.

Is this, my golden voice, reduced to dross?
My loss, the world's; my stage now confined
to pantomimist's arts. My role's the fool,
the butt, the simpleton, the bell-bedazzled jester,
the clown.

A comedown complete and yet ever so neat —
a fortuitous topple from fire-pressure heights of
fame,
where a rebel reveled in the drooling depths of
critics' praises,
admired the throngs that flocked to cruel seas,
flattered pusillanimous ghosts at the B.B.C.,
and tweaked the world from Drury, Kwai, to Israel
and Innisfail.

So hard the climb, so hardened to success,
the Medusa fingers of two-faced Fate,
a triumph of Life's nothingness!

What years of patronized torment lie ahead
until diminishing contracts force my buffoonish
acts

to bottoms of the bills?
Numbed, am I painlessly re-born,
one forlorn, freakish, Fawkesian guy,
a miming mummer of another's words,
dubbed with the curling chords
of some second-rate ham.

APPENDIX FOUR

A Pathetic Story

by Jerome K. Jerome

"Oh! I want you to write the pathetic story for the Christmas number, if you will, old man," said the editor of the *Family Circle Weekly Journal* to me, as I poked my head into his den one sunny July morning, some years ago. "Thomas is anxious to have the comic sketch. He says he overheard a joke last week, that he thinks he can work up. I expect I myself shall have to do the cheerful love story, about the man that everybody thinks is dead and that turns up on Christmas-eve and marries the girl. I was hoping to get out of it this time, but I'm afraid I can't. Then I shall get Miggs to do the charitable appeal business. I think he's the most experienced man we have now for that; and Skittles can run off the cynical column, about the Christmas bills, and the indigestion; he's always very good in a cynical article, Skittles is; he's got just the correct don't-know-what-he-means-himself sort of touch for it, if you understand."

"Skittles", I may mention, was the nickname we have given to a singularly emotional and seriously inclined member of the staff, whose correct cognomen was Beherhend.

Skittles himself always waxed particularly sentimental over Christmas. During the week preceding that sacred festival, he used to go about literally swelling with geniality and affection for all man and womankind. He would greet comparative strangers with a burst of delight that other men would have found difficult to work up in the case of a rich relation, and would shower upon them the good wishes, always so plentiful and cheap at that season, with such an evident conviction that practical benefit to the wishee would ensue therefrom as to send them away laboring under a vague sense of obligation.

The sight of an old friend at that period was dangerous to him. His feelings would quite overcome him. He could not speak. You feared that he would burst.

He was generally quite laid up on Christmas-day itself, owing to having drunk so many sentimental toasts on Christmas-eve. I never saw such a man as Skittles for proposing and drinking sentimental toasts. He would drink to "dear old Christmas-time," and to "dear old England;" and then he would drink to his mother, and all his other relations, and to "lovely woman," and "old chums," or he would propose "Friendship," in the abstract, "may it never grow cool in the heart of a true-born Briton," and "Love— may it ever look out at us from the eyes of our sweethearts and wives," or even "the Sun—that is ever shining behind the clouds, dear boys,—where we can't see it, and where it is not of much use to us." He was so full of sentiment, was Skittles!

But his favorite toast, and the one over which he would become more eloquently lugubrious than over any other, was always "absent friends." He appeared to be singularly rich in "absent friends." And it must be said for him that he never forgot them. Whenever and wherever liquor was to his hand, Skittles's "absent friends" were sure of a drink, and his present friends, unless they displayed great tact and firmness, of a speech calculated to give them all the blues

108

for a week.

Folks did say at one time that Skittles's eyes usually turned in the direction of the county jail when he pledged this toast; but on its being ascertained that Skittles's kindly remembrance was not intended to be exclusive, but embraced everybody else's absent friends as well as his own, the uncharitable suggestion was withdrawn.

Still, we had too much of these "absent friends," however comprehensive a body they may have been. Skittles overdid the business. We all think highly of our friends when they are absent,—more highly, as a rule, than we do of them when they are not absent. But we do not want to be always worrying about them. At a Christmas party, or a complimentary dinner to somebody, or at a shareholders' meeting, where you naturally feel good and sad, they are in place, but Skittles dragged them in at the most inappropriate seasons. Never shall I forget his proposing their health once at a wedding. It had been a jolly wedding. Everything had gone off splendidly, and everybody was in the best of spirits. The breakfast was over, and quite all the necessary toasts had been drunk. It was getting near the time for the bride and bridegroom to depart, and we were just thinking about collecting the rice and boots with which to finally bless them, when Skittles rose in his place, with a funereal expression on his countenance and a glass of wine in his hand.

I guessed what was coming in a moment. I tried to kick him under the table. I do not mean, of course, that I tried to kick him there altogether; though I am not at all sure whether, under the circumstances, I should not have been justified in going even to that length. What I mean is, that the attempt to kick him took place under the table.

It failed, however. True, I did kick somebody; but it evidently could not have been Skittles, for he remained unmoved. In all probability it was the bride, who was sitting next to him. I did not try again; and he started, uninterfered with, on his favorite theme.

"Friends," he commenced, his voice trembling with emotion, while a tear glistened in his eye, "before we part—some of us, perhaps, never to meet again on earth—before this guileless young couple, who have this day taken upon themselves the manifold trials and troubles of married life, quit the peaceful fold, as it were, to face the bitter griefs and disappointments of this weary life, there is one toast, hitherto undrunk, that I would wish to propose."

Here he wiped away the before-mentioned tear, and the people looked solemn, and endeavored to crack nuts without making a noise.

"Friends," he went on, growing more and more impressive and dejected in his tones, "there are few of us here who have not at some time or other known what it is to lose, through death or travel, a dear beloved one—maybe two or three."

At this point, he stifled a sob; and the bridegroom's aunt, at the bottom of the table, whose eldest son had lately left the country at the expense of his relations, upon the clear understanding that he would never again return, began to cry quietly into the rice-pudding.

"The fair young maiden at my side," continued Skittles, clearing his throat, and laying his hand tenderly on the bride's shoulder, "as you are all aware, was, a few years ago, bereft of her mother. Ladies and gentlemen, what can be more sad than the death of a mother?" This, of course, had the effect of starting the bride off sobbing. The bridegroom, meaning well, but, naturally, under the circumstances, nervous and excited, sought to console her by murmuring that he felt sure it had all happened for the best, and that no one who had ever known the old lady would for a moment wish her back again; upon which he was indignantly informed by his newly-made wife that if he was so very pleased at her mother's death, it was a pity he had not told her so before, and she would never have married him—and he sank into thoughtful silence.

On my looking up, which I had hitherto carefully abstained from doing, my eyes unfortunately encountered those of a brother journalist who was sitting at the other side of the table, and we both burst out laughing, thereupon gaining a reputation for callousness that I do not suppose either of us has outlived to this day.

Skittles, the only human being at that once festive board that did not appear to be wishing he were any-where else, droned on, with evident satisfaction: "Friends," he said, "shall that dear mother be forgotten at this joyous gathering? Shall the lost mother, father, brother, sister, child, friend of any of us be forgotten? No, ladies and gentlemen! Let us, amid our merriment, still think of those lost, wandering souls: let us, amid the wine-cup and the blithesome jest, remember—Absent Friends."

The toast was drunk to the accompaniment of suppressed sobs and low moans, and the wedding guests left the table to bathe their faces and calm their thoughts. The bride, rejecting the proffered assistance of the groom, was assisted into the carriage by her father, and departed, evidently full of misgivings as to her chance of future happiness in the society of such a heartless monster as her husband had just shown himself to be.

Skittles has been an "absent friend" himself at that house ever since.

But I am not getting on with my pathetic story.

"Do not be late with it," our editor had said. "Let me have it by the end of August, certain. I mean to be early with the Christmas number this time. We didn't get it out till October last year, you know. I don't want the *Clipper* to be before us again!"

"Oh, that will be all right," I had answered, airily. "I shall soon run that off. I've nothing much to do this week. I'll start it at once."

So, as I went home, I cast about in my mind for a pathetic subject to work on. But not a pathetic idea could I think of. Comic fancies crowded in upon me, until my brain began to give way under the strain of holding them; and, if I had not calmed myself down with a last week's *Punch*, I should, in all probability, have gone off in a fit.

"Oh, I'm evidently not in the humor for pathos," I said to myself. "It is no use trying to force it. I've got plenty of time. I will wait till I feel sad."

But as the days went on, I merely grew more and more cheerful. By the middle of August, matters were becoming serious. If I could not, by some means or other, contrive to get myself into a state of the blues during the next week or ten days, there would be nothing in the Christmas number of the *Family Circle Weekly Journal* to make the British public wretched, and its reputation as a high-class paper for home and family would be irretrievably ruined!

I was a conscientious young man in those days. I had undertaken to write a four-and-a-half column pathetic story by the end of August; and if—no matter at what mental or physical cost to myself—the task could be accomplished, those four columns and a half would be ready.

I have generally found indigestion a good breeder of sorrowful thoughts. Accordingly, for a couple of days I lived upon an exclusive diet of hot boiled pork, Yorkshire pudding, and assorted pastry, with lobster salad for supper. It gave me comic nightmares. I dreamed of elephants trying to climb trees, and of churchwardens being caught playing pitch-and-toss on Sundays, and woke up shaking with laughter!

I abandoned the dyspeptic scheme, and took to reading all the pathetic literature I could collect together. But it was of no use. The little girl in Wordsworth's "We Are Seven" only irritated me; I wanted to slap her. Byron's blighted pirates bored me. When, in a novel, the heroine died, I was glad; and when the author told me that the hero never smiled again on earth, I did not believe it.

As a last resource, I re-perused one or two of my own concoctions. They made me feel ashamed of myself, but not exactly miserable—at least, not miserable in the way I wanted to be miserable.

Then I bought all the standard works of wit and humor that had ever been published, and waded steadily through the lot. They lowered me a good deal, but not sufficiently. My cheerfulness seemed proof against everything.

One Saturday evening I went out and hired a man to come in and sing sentimental ballads to me. He earned his money (five shillings). He sang me everything dismal there was in English, Scotch, Irish, and Welsh, together with a few translations from the German; and, after the first hour and a half, I found myself unconsciously trying to dance to the different tunes. I invented some really pretty steps for "Auld Robin Grey," winding up with a quaint flourish of the left leg at the end of each verse.

At the beginning of the last week, I went to my editor and laid the case before him.

"Why, what's the matter with you?" he said. "You used to be so good at that sort of thing! Have you thought of the poor girl who loves the young man that goes away and never comes back, and she waits and waits, and never marries, and nobody knows that her heart is breaking?"

"Of course I have!" I retorted, rather irritably. "Do you think I don't know the rudiments of my profession?"

"Well," he remarked, "won't it do?"

"No," I answered. "With marriage such a failure as it seems to be all round now-a-days, how can you pump up sorrow for anyone lucky enough to keep out of it?"

"Um," he mused, "how about the child that tells everybody not to cry, and then dies?"

"Oh, and a good riddance to it!" I replied, peevishly. "There are too many children in this world. Look what a noise they make, and what a lot of money they cost in boots!"

My editor agreed that I did not appear to be in the proper spirit to write a pathetic child-story.

He inquired if I had thought of the old man who wept over the faded love-letters on Christmas-eve; and I said that I had, and that I considered him an old idiot.

"Would a dog story do?" he continued: "something about a dead dog; that's always popular."

"Not Christmassy enough," I argued.

The betrayed maiden was suggested; but dismissed, on reflection, as being too broad a subject for the pages of a "Companion for Home and Hearth"—our sub-title.

"Well, think it over for another day," said my editor. "I don't want to have to go to Jenks. He can only be pathetic as a costermonger, and our lady readers don't always like the expressions."

I thought I would go and ask the advice of a friend of mine—a very famous and popular author; in fact, one of the *most* famous and popular authors of the day. I was very proud of his friendship, because he was a very great man indeed: not great, perhaps, in the earnest meaning of the word; not great like the greatest men—the men who do not know that they are great—but decidedly great, according to the practical standard. When he wrote a book, a hundred thousand copies would be sold during the first week; and when a play of his was produced, the theatre was crammed for five hundred nights. And of each new work it was said that it was more clever and grand and glorious than were even the works he had written before.

Wherever the English language was spoken, his name was an honored household word. Wherever he went, he was fêted and lionised and cheered. Descriptions of his charming house, of his charming sayings and doings, of his charming self, were in every newspaper.

Shakespeare was not one-half so famous in his day as XX is in his.

Fortunately, he happened to be still in town; and on being ushered into his sumptuously-furnished study, I found him sitting before one of the windows, smoking an after-dinner cigar.

He offered me one from the same box. XX's cigars are not to be refused. I know he pays half-a-crown a-piece for them by the hundred; so I accepted, lit up, and, sitting down opposite to him, told him my trouble.

He did not answer immediately after I had finished; and I was just beginning to think that he could not have been listening, when—with his eyes looking out through the open window to where, beyond the smoky city, it seemed as if the sun, in passing through, had left the gates of the sky ajar behind him—he took his cigar from his lips, and said:

"Do you want a real pathetic story? I can tell you one if you do. It is not very long, but it is sad enough."

He spoke in so serious a tone that almost any reply seemed out of place, and I remained silent.

"It is the story of a man who lost his own self," he continued, still looking out upon the dying light, as though he read the story there, "who stood by the death-bed of himself, and saw himself slowly die, and knew that he was dead—for ever."

Once upon a time there lived a poor boy. He had little in common with other children. He loved to wander by himself, to think and dream all day. It was not that he was morose, or did not care for his comrades, only that something within kept whispering to his childish heart that he had deeper lessons to comprehend than his schoolmates had. And an unseen hand would lead him away into the solitude where alone he could learn their meaning.

Ever amid the babel of the swarming street, would he hear strong, silent voices, speaking to him as he walked, telling him of the work that would one day be entrusted to his hands,—work for God, such as is given to only the very few to do, work for the helping of God's children in the world, for the making of them stronger and truer and higher;—and, in some dimly-lighted corner, where for a moment they were alone, he would stand and raise his boyish hands to heaven, and thank God for this great promised gift of noble usefulness, and pray that he might ever prove worthy of the trust; and, in the joy of his coming work, the little frets of life floated like drift-wood on a deepening river; and as he grew, the voices spoke to him ever more plainly, until he saw his work before him clearly, as a traveler on the hill-top sees the pathway through the vale.

And so the years passed, and he became a man, and his labor lay ready to his hand.

And then a foul demon came and tempted him—the demon that has killed many a better man before, that will kill many a great man yet—the demon of worldly success. And the demon whispered evil words into his ear, and, God forgive him!—he listened.

"Of what good to *you*, think you, will it be, your writing mighty truths and noble thoughts? What will the world pay for *them*? What has ever been the reward of the earth's greatest teachers and poets—the men who have given their lives to the best service of mankind—but neglect and scorn and poverty? Look around! what are the wages of the few earnest workers of to-day but a pauper's pittance, compared with the wealth that is showered down on those who jig to the tune that the crowd shouts for? Aye, the true singers are honored when they are dead—those that are remembered; and the thoughts from their brains once fallen, whether they themselves are remembered or not, stir, with ever-widening circles to all time, the waters of human life. But of what use is that to themselves, who starved? You have talent, genius. Riches, luxury, power can be yours—soft beds and dainty foods. You can be great in the greatness that the world can see, famous with the fame your own ears will hear. Work for the world, and the world will pay you promptly; the wages the gods give are long delayed."

And the demon prevailed over him, and he fell.

And, instead of being the servant of God, he became the slave of men. And he wrote for the multitude what they wanted to hear, and the multitude applauded and flung money to him, and as he would stoop to pick it up, he would grin and touch his cap, and tell them how generous and noble they were.

And the spirit of the artist that is handmaiden to the spirit of the prophet departed from him, and he grew into the clever huckster, the smart tradesman, whose only desire was to discover the public taste that he might pander to it.

"Only tell me what it is you like," he would cry in his heart, "that I may write it for you, good people! Will you have again the old lies? Do you still love the old dead conventions, the worn-out formulas of life, the rotting weeds of evil thoughts that keep the fresh air from the flowers?

"Shall I sing again to you the childish twaddle you have heard a million times before? Shall I defend for you the wrong, and call it right? Shall I stab Truth in the back for you, or praise it?

"How shall I flatter you to-day, and in what way to-morrow and the next day? Only tell me what you wish me to say, what you wish me to think, that I may say it and think it, good people, and so get your pence and your plaudits!"

Thus he became rich and famous and great; and had fine clothes to wear and rich foods to eat, as the demon had promised him, and servants to wait on him, and horses, and carriages to ride in; and he would have been happy—as happy as such things can make a man—only that at the bottom of his desk there lay (and he had never had the courage to destroy them) a little pile of faded manuscripts, written in a boyish hand, that would speak to him of the memory of a poor lad who had once paced the city's feet-worn stones, dreaming of no other greatness than that of being one of God's messengers to men, and who had died, and had been buried for all eternity, long years ago.

It was a very sad story, but not exactly the sort of sad story, I felt, the public wants in a Christmas number. So I had to fall back on the broken-hearted maiden, after all!

COMMENTS

You now have a pretty good idea at least of the qualities I look for in short prose and poetry. You've also had a taste of my own work and have just read a piece by Jerome K. Jerome, which I regard as the finest short story in the English language.

Or is *A Pathetic Story* a short story? Perhaps it's better described as an essay. In any event, it's a piece that appears to break all the rules of story or essay construction. The narrative seems to wander all over the place—and that is exactly the sort of free-flowing, fluid impression Jerome strives to give. In actual fact, a closer examination reveals that the story has been very carefully and meticulously built up along the same classical lines we've been discussing all along: A good opening, using dialogue that draws the reader straight into the picture and lays the foundation for the whole work in the very first sentence.

And right from the jump, Jerome introduces potential conflict. We all expect the too-ready-to-oblige, airily dismissive journalist (who is actually Jerome himself as illustrations in the original work make clear) will be obliged to confront more than a few troublesome hurdles in fulfilling his assignment. For one thing, he patently lacks concentration. Off on a tangent, he seemingly goes, picking up a cue from the long-winded editor to tell us a series of anecdotes involving the genial Skittles and his "absent friends".

Actually, from a modern point of view, *Absent Friends* would make a better title for the story. Of course, in Jerome's day, "pathetic" did not carry the derogatory label it has now.

In any event, the idea of loss, being fundamental to the story, is pointedly and masterfully introduced right from the start and then brilliantly carried through to a triple whammy conclusion.

But it's not just Jerome's mastery of technique I admire, nor even his prescient ability to expatiate upon themes and hit upon allusions that are still so true and familiar today (the story was written some 120 years ago), but the direct appeal he makes to the emotions. Jerome makes me laugh, he makes me cry. He leads me into a familiar but secret world. He makes me gasp in wonder. He teaches me the fundamental essence of truth and life. He points a way that fills me with an intense desire to follow.

Submit a short story as artistically crafted, as funny, as allusive, as poignant, as true-to-life as a re-titled *Absent Friends*, and you'll certainly have the winners' circle in your sights, and maybe First Prize in your pocket.

And now, back to Poetry…

The Bells

translated by **John Howard Reid**

I hear them, I love them
as I hear the rumor of the wind,
the murmur of the fountain,
or the bellow of a lamb.

Just as birds caw and cry,
soaring in the sky to greet
the first gleam of dawn,
so the bells scan the hills with their echoes.

As their tongues pound the plains,
their tones linger long in the valleys
with voices of candor,
of peace and endearment.

Should our bells become forever silenced,
what sadness permeates the air and sky!
what oppressive stillness haunts our churches!
and how thunderstruck are the village dead!

Translated from the Castilian of Rosalia

A King of the Goths

translated by **John Howard Reid**

Although you may be heir to the noblest lands,
adorn your arms with the spoils of Egyptian palaces,
drink barbaric wines from Chaldean chalices
and hold all the loot of Rome in your hands;

although you may throw a sultan's treasure in the temple bowl,
burn Asia's richest incense, clothe priests with Mexican plumes,
shower slaves with the wealth of pyramids, their wives—
Arabian perfumes,
and spread the fame of your name from Pole to Pole;

although a circlet of laurel your brow is swathing,
the wheel of Fortune your eyes are guiding,
the laws of the world your whims deciding;

although crowned kings at your voice are trembling,
and on the forehead of the moon your feet are treading,
if you lack virtue, you have nothing.

Translated from the Spanish of Lupercio Leonardo de Argensola

The Miner

by **James Russell Lowell**

Down 'mid the tangled roots of things
That coil about the central fire,
I seek for that which giveth wings
To stoop, not soar, to my desire.

Sometimes I hear, as 'twere a sigh,
The sea's deep yearning far above,
"Thou hast the secret not," I cry,
"In deeper deeps is hid my Love."

They think I burrow from the sun,
In darkness, all alone, and weak;
Such loss were gain if He were won,
For 'tis the sun's own Sun I seek.

"The earth," they murmur, "is the tomb
That vainly sought His life to prison;
Why grovel longer in the gloom?
He is not here; He hath arisen."

More life for me where He hath lain
Hidden while ye believed Him dead,
Than in cathedrals cold and vain,
Built on loose sands of IT IS SAID.

My search is for the living gold;
Him I desire who dwells recluse,
And not His image worn and old,
Day-servant of our sordid use.

If Him I find not, yet I find
The ancient joy of cell and church,
The glimpse, the surety undefined,
The unquenched ardour of the search.

Happier to chase a flying goal
Than to sit counting laurelled gains,
To guess the soul within the soul
Than to be lord of what remains.

Hide still, best Good, in subtile wise,
Beyond my nature's utmost scope;
Be ever absent from mine eyes
To be twice present in my hope!

The Jackdaw of Rheims

by **Reverend Richard Harris Barham**

The Jackdaw sat on the Cardinal's chair!
Bishop and abbot and prior were there;
     Many a monk and many a friar,
     Many a knight, and many a squire,
With a great many more of lesser degree, —
In sooth a goodly company;
And they served the Lord Primate on bended knee.
     Never, I ween,   Was a prouder seen,
Read of in books, or dreamt of in dreams,
Than the Cardinal Lord Archbishop of Rheims!

     In and out   Through the motley rout,
That little Jackdaw kept hopping about;
     Here and there   Like a dog in a fair,
     Over comfits and cates,   And dishes and plates,
Cowl and cope, and rochet and pall,
Mitre and crosier! he hopp'd upon all!
     With a saucy air,   He perch'd on the chair
Where, in state, the great Lord Cardinal sat
In the great Lord Cardinal's great red hat;
     And he peer'd in the face   Of his Lordship's Grace,
With a satisfied look, as if he would say,
"We two are the greatest folk here today!"
     And the priests, with awe,   As such freaks they saw,
Said, "The Devil must be in that little Jackdaw!"

The feast was over, the board was clear'd,
The flawns and the custard had all disappear'd,

And six little Singing-boys, —dear little souls!
In nice clean faces, and nice white stoles,
      Came in order due, Two by two,
Marching that grand refectory through!
A nice little boy held a golden ewer,
Emboss'd and fill'd with water, as pure
As any that flows between Rheims and Namur,
Which a nice little boy stood ready to catch
In a fine golden hand-basin made to match.
Two nice little boys, rather more grown,
Carried lavender-water and eau de Cologne;
And a nice little boy had a nice cake of soap,
Worthy of washing the hands of the Pope.
      One little boy more A napkin bore,
Of the best white diaper, fringed with pink,
Picturing a Cardinal's Hat in "permanent ink."

The great Lord Cardinal turns at the sight
Of these nice little boys dress'd all in white:
      From his finger he draws His costly turquoise;
And, not thinking at all about little Jackdaws,
      Deposits it straight By the side of his plate,
While the nice little boys on his Eminence wait;
Till, when nobody's dreaming of any such thing,
That unseen Jackdaw makes off with the ring!

      There's a cry and a shout, And a deuce of a rout,
And nobody seems to know what they're about,
But the monks have their pockets all turned inside out,
      The friars are kneeling, And hunting, and feeling
The carpet, the walls, and the floor and the ceiling.
      The Cardinal drew Off each plum-colored shoe,
And left his red stockings exposed to the view.
      He peeps, and he feels In the toes and the heels;

They turn up the dishes, they turn up the plates,
They take up the poker and poke out the grates,
> They turn up the rugs,   They examine the mugs:
> But, no! No such thing: They can't find THE
RING!
And the Abbot declared that, "when nobody twigg'd it,
Some rascal or other had popp'd in, and prigg'd it!"

The Cardinal rose with a dignified look,
He call'd for his candle, his bell, and his book!
> In holy anger, and pious grief,
> He solemnly cursed that rascally thief!
> He cursed him at board, he cursed him in bed;
> From the sole of his foot to the crown of his head;
> He cursed him in sleeping, that every night
> He should dream of the devil, and wake in a fright;
> He cursed him in eating, he cursed him in drinking,
> He cursed him in coughing, in sneezing, in winking;
> He cursed him in sitting, in standing, in lying;
> He cursed him in walking, in riding, in flying,
> He cursed him in living, he cursed him dying!
Never was heard such a terrible curse!
> But what gave rise   To no little surprise,
Nobody seem'd one penny the worse!

> The day was gone,   The night came on,
The monks and the friars they search'd till dawn;
> When the Sacristan saw,   On crumpled claw,
Come limping a poor little lame Jackdaw!
> No longer gay,   As on yesterday;
His feathers all seem'd to be turn'd the wrong way;
His pinions droop'd—he could hardly stand,—
His head was as bald as the palm of your hand.
> His eye so dim,   So wasted each limb,
That, heedless of grammar, they all cried, "THAT"S HIM!
That's the scamp that has done this scandalous thing!

That's the thief that filched my Lord Cardinal's ring!"
　　　　The poor little Jackdaw,　When the monks he saw,
Feebly gave vent to the ghost of a caw;
And turn'd his bald head, as much to say,
"Pray be so good as to walk this way!"
Slower and slower he limp'd on before,
Till they came to the back of the belfry door,
　　　　Where the first thing they saw,　Midst the sticks
and the straw,
Was the RING in the nest of that little Jackdaw!

Then the great Lord Cardinal call'd for his book,
And off that terrible curse he took;
　　　　The mute expression　Served in lieu of confession,
And, being thus coupled with full restitution,
The Jackdaw receiv'd a Plenary Absolution!
　　　　When those words were heard,　That poor little bird
Was so changed in a moment, 'twas really absurd:
　　　　He grew sleek, and fat;　In addition to that,
A fresh crop of feathers came thick as a mat!

　　　　His tail wagged more　Even more than before;
But no longer it wagged with an impudent air,
No longer he perch'd on the Cardinal's chair.
　　　　He hopp'd now about　With a gait devout;
At Matins, at Vespers, he never was out;
And, so far from any more pilfering deeds,
He always seem'd telling the Confessor's beads.

If anyone lied, of if anyone swore,
Or slumber'd in prayer-time and happen'd to snore,
　　　　That good Jackdaw　Would cry a great "Caw!"
As much as to say, "Don't do that any more!"
While many remark'd, as his manners they saw,
That they "never had known such a pious Jackdaw!"

He long lived the pride   Of that countryside,
And at last in the odor of sanctity died;
    When, as words were too faint,   His merits to paint,
The Conclave determined to make him a Saint;
And on newly-made Saints and Popes, as you know,
It's the custom, at Rome, new names to bestow,
So they canonized him by the name Jem Crow!

Elegy Written in a Country Churchyard

by **Thomas Gray**

The Curfew tolls the knell of parting day,
  The lowing herd wind slowly o'er the lea,
The plowman homeward plods his weary way,
  And leaves the world to darkness and to me.

Him have we seen the greenwood side along,
  When o'er the heath we hied, our labor done,
Oft as the woodlark piped her farewell song,
  With wistful eyes pursue the setting sun.

Now fades the glimmering landscape on the sight,
  And all the air a solemn stillness holds,
Save where the beetle wheels his droning flight,
  And drowsy tinklings lull the distant folds;

Save that from yonder ivy-mantled tow'r
  The moping owl does to the moon complain
Of such, as wand'ring near her secret bow'r,
  Molest her ancient solitary reign.

Beneath those rugged elms, that yew tree's shade,
  Where heaves the turf in many a mould'ring heap,
Each in his narrow cell forever laid,
  The rude Forefathers of the hamlet sleep.

The breezy call of incense-bearing Morn,
  The swallow twitt'ring from the straw-built shed,
The cock's shrill clarion, or the echoing horn,
  No more shall rouse them from their lowly bed.

For them no more the blazing hearth shall burn,
  Or busy housewife ply her evening care:
  No children run to lisp their sire's return,
Or climb his knees the envied kiss to share.

Oft did the harvest to their sickle yield,
  The furrow oft the stubborn glebe has broke;
How jocund did they drive their team afield!
  How bow'd the woods beneath their sturdy stroke!

Let not Ambition mock their useful toil,
  Their homely joys, and destiny obscure;
Nor Grandeur hear with a disdainful smile
  The short and simple annals of the poor.

The boast of heraldry, the pomp of pow'r,
  And all that beauty, all that wealth e'er gave,
Awaits alike th' inevitable hour.
  The paths of glory lead but to the grave.

Nor you, ye Proud, impute to These the fault,
  If Mem'ry o'er their Tomb no trophies raise,
Where thro' the long-drawn aisle and fretted vault
  The pealing anthem swells the note of praise.

Can storied urn or animated bust
  Back to its mansion call the fleeting breath?
Can Honor's voice provoke the silent dust,
  Or Flatt'ry soothe the dull cold ear of Death?

Perhaps in this neglected spot is laid
    Some heart once pregnant with celestial fire;
Hands, that the rod of empire might have sway'd,
    Or wak'd to ecstasy the living lyre.

But Knowledge to their eyes her ample page
    Rich with the spoils of Time did ne'er unroll;
Chill Penury repress'd their noble rage,
    And froze the genial current of the soul.

Full many a gem of purest ray serene,
    The dark unfathom'd caves of ocean bear:
Full many a flower is born to blush unseen
    And waste its sweetness on the desert air.

Some village-Hampden that with dauntless breast
    The little Tyrant of his fields withstood;
Some mute inglorious Milton here may rest,
    Some Cromwell guiltless of his country's blood.

Th' applause of list'ning Senates to command,
    The threats of pain and ruin to despise,
To scatter plenty o'er a smiling land,
    And read their hist'ry in a nation's eyes, —

Their lot forbade: nor circumscrib'd alone
    Their growing virtues, but their crimes confin'd;
Forbade to wade through slaughter to a throne,
    And shut the gates of mercy on mankind;

The struggling pangs of conscious truth to hide,
    To quench the blushes of ingenuous shame,
Or heap the shrine of Luxury and Pride
    With incense kindled at the Muse's flame.

The thoughtless world to Majesty may bow,
    Exalt the brave, and idolize Success;
But more to Innocence their safety owe
    Than Power or Genius e'er conspired to bless.

And thou, who, mindful of th' unhonored Dead,
    Dost in these notes their artless tale relate,
By night and lonely contemplation led
    To wander in the gloomy walks of Fate:

Hark how the sacred calm that breathes around
    Bids every fierce tumultuous passion cease;
In still small accents whisp'ring from the ground
    A grateful earnest of eternal Peace.

No more with Reason and thyself at strife,
    Give anxious cares and endless wishes room,
But thro' the cool sequestered vale of life
    Pursue the silent tenor of thy doom.

Far from the madding crowd's ignoble strife,
    Their sober wishes never learned to stray;
Along the cool sequester'd vale of life
    They kept the noiseless tenor of their way.

Yet ev'n these bones some insult to protect
    Some frail memorial still erected nigh,
With uncouth rhymes and shameless sculpture deck'd
    Implores the passing tribute of a sigh.

Their name, their years, spelt by th' unlettered muse,
    The place of fame and elegy supply;
And many a holy text around she strews
    That teach the rustic moralist to die.

For who, to dumb Forgetfulness a prey,
    This pleasing anxious being e'er resigned,
Left the warm precincts of the cheerful day,
    Nor cast one longing ling'ring look behind?

On some fond breast the parting soul relies,
    Some pious drops the closing eye requires;
Ev'n from the tomb the voice of Nature cries,
    Ev'n in our Ashes live their wonted Fires.

Haply some hoary-headed Swain may say,
    "Oft have we seen him at the peep of dawn
Brushing with hasty steps the dews away
    To meet the sun upon the upland lawn.

"There at the foot of yonder nodding beech
    That wreathes its old fantastic roots so high,
His listless length at noontide would he stretch,
    And pore upon the brook that babbles by.

"Hard by yon wood, now smiling as in scorn,
    Mutt'ring his wayward fancies he would rove,
Now dropping, woeful wan, like one forlorn,
    Or craz'd with care, or cross'd in hopeless love.

"One morn I miss'd him on the custom'd hill,
    Along the heath and near his fav'rite tree,
Another came; nor yet beside the rill,
    Nor up the lawn, nor at the wood was he;

"The next with dirges due in sad array
    Slow thro' the church-way path we saw him borne.
Approach and read (for thou canst read) the lay,
    Grav'd on the stone beneath yon aged thorn.

"There scattered oft, the earliest of the year,
  By hands unseen are show'rs of violets found;
The redbreast loves to build and warble there,
  And little footsteps lightly print the ground."

THE EPITAPH

Here rests his head upon the lap of Earth,
  A youth to Fortune and to Fame unknown.
Fair Science frowned not on his humble birth.
  And Melancholy mark'd him for her own.

Large was his bounty, and his soul sincere,
  Heav'n did a recompense as largely send:
He gave to Mis'ry all he had, a tear;
  He gain'd from Heaven ('twas all he wish'd) a friend.

No farther seek his merits to disclose,
  Or draw his frailties from their dread abode,
(There they alike in trembling hope repose),
  The bosom of his Father and his God.

What is Poetry?

Some guidelines for entering the Tom Howard Poetry Contest

I enjoy judging poetry. It's a snack compared to reading other forms of literature. A story may start poorly, but soon develop into a fascinating character study, a fanciful adventure, an engrossing slice-of-life, or even a riotous comedy. But poetry, you need to read only a stanza or two and you know instantly whether it's going to make the grade to WORTH FURTHER READING or pop instantly into the REJECT basket.

We critics can argue from now to Doomsday as to what exactly poetry is. But we all agree on what it is not. I believe poetry can be and should be anything and everything: A vehicle for ideas, a simple description, an emotion, a thought, a time capsule, a conversation, a tirade and even a story or straight narrative. *The moon was a ghostly galleon, tossed upon cloudy seas; the road was a ribbon of moonlight across the dusty moor; and the highwayman came riding, riding, up to the old inn door.* I don't care that narrative poems are now out of style. If Alfred Noyes can do it, so can you.

Incidentally, I regard *The Highwayman* as the finest narrative poem in English. I intended to print it here so that all could admire it anew. But, although published over a hundred years ago, *The Highwayman* is still under copyright. Not that I object to paying a fee. The problem is (a) to discover who is the present owner and (b) to negotiate with the owner's representative. This can take considerable time—anything from six months to six years!

Getting back to judging for the moment, I have only one bugaboo. Only one. I will not tolerate doggerel. All other forms, types, genres of verse are welcome. But I don't consider doggerel "poetry". It's just plain simple rubbish.

136

So what exactly is doggerel? My dictionary says "bad verse." So what makes it bad? In a word: clichés. In doggerel, June always rhymes with moon, never with bassoon or octoroon; love is almost always coupled with above, rarely with shove or glove. Doggerel forms a compulsory ingredient of greeting cards. *A warm hello, a friendly smile, a word of cheer, and then...A special wish that you will soon be feeling well again!* By the humble standards of doggerel, that's actually not too excruciating, but it's still an inevitable candidate for the recycle bin.

Would you believe that 95% of my instant rejects belong to the doggerel class of poetry entries? 95%! I blame the internet's multitudinous, non-discriminatory web sites for this sudden rise in the popularity of instant trash. I want no part of it. Yet budding poets will insist on entering this garbage by the truckload. A complete waste of money. There's no way I'd award *A warm hello* a single cent, let alone a thousand dollars.

The worst offenders are amateur religious poets. *I pray to Jesus night and day. He listens hard to what I say.* I'm sure he does! But I'm also sure he's none too thrilled by this insensitive poet's lack of care and creativity.

Next in line are the romantic poets. The moon in June brigade. Running a close third are the philosophers. *The world would be a better place, I think it would be too, if only all the human race, would to themselves be true!*

If you must use rhyming verse, for God's sake, be original!

So what distinguishes good poetry from good prose? To my mind, the answer is *selectivity*. In prose, the primary function of a word is to convey a meaning. And unless you're a slapdash prose-writer like Harold Robbins or Sir Walter Scott, you will do your best to select the most appropriate word that contains the exact shading you wish to convey.

In poetry, however, meaning is just one of several functions. Take two famous lines from Gray's *Elegy*:

The thoughtless world to Majesty may bow,
Exalt the brave, and idolize Success.

Why not *The heedless mob may bend their knees to the rich, the powerful, the successful and the well-connected*? That makes as much sense. Perhaps more. But Gray's words are chosen not just for their meaning, but for their rhythm, their metrical and rhyming patterns, and perhaps above all for their ability to form a picture, a lasting image in our minds. Why are Gray's words easier to remember, and more pleasing, more harmonious than my paraphrase?

Even if we dispense with rhymes and throw meter to the wind, we still need to make our poetry special. It has to have something that prose doesn't normally have. Even a prose poem must employ some arrangement that makes it stand out. A poem must also be many-layered. It must reveal its main thrust on a first reading, but not all its secrets. It must keep some shades and insights in reserve for a second and third reading.

To achieve the ultimate goal of First, Second or Third Prize, a poem must also have a quality that makes it stand out above the rest. This is the quality a reader looks for in great poetry. In Gray's *Elegy* the poet uses a theme with which we can all identify and casts it with memorable images. So abundantly rich, in fact, is Gray's verse that both the poet and his editors could afford to discard a few stanzas from edition to edition. However, I love them all. I couldn't bear to lose *idolize Success* or the plowman's *greenwood* or the redbreast's *little footsteps*. So I have printed the poem in full.

Although short, Lowell's *The Miner* is a brilliant example of a many-layered poem. It's perfectly natural for the reader to accept the narrator as *the miner* on a first reading. It's not until the third or fourth perusal that you realize *you* are the miner. Notice also how Lowell very cleverly seduces us in the first stanzas into an expectation that he is going to trot out all the usual religious effigies and dogmas. What a surprise when he attacks the very institutions he ostensibly sets out to praise!

Barham's satirical *Jackdaw* has garnered a few thin-skinned detractors, but it's a friendly, jovial satire in which the poet very adroitly ridicules church dignity. His lines have plenty of sting but—to my mind, at least—they don't give offense.

Winning poems all have one quality in common: Originality! I recommend that quality to you: **ORIGINALITY!**

POSTSCRIPT

Quite some years ago, I was the keynote speaker at a Literary Luncheon organized by one of the country's leading writers' associations. The wife of the then Prime Minister was present, as she was the Patron of that society. The President asked her if she would care to be introduced to me and she replied in a loud voice that the whole table could hear: "Indeed not! I abhor crime writing!"

I was tempted to reply, "In that case, you've never read any of the world's masters like Dickens or Conrad, Homer or Shakespeare, Steinbeck or Faulkner, Dostoevsky or Poe, Hugo or Tolstoy, Hawthorne or Stevenson." But rather than cause a ruckus at the main table, I kept silent.

Until recently, I deluded myself that such ideas were now out of date. But, alas, I was mistaken. They are still very much present. How often do you see a major literary award offered to a writer of genre fiction or comic verse?

The main reason behind establishing the Tom Howard Contests for poetry and prose, was to provide a level playing field that would not discriminate against detective fiction, or science fiction, or romantic fiction, or humorous poems and parodies. Oddly, few writers in these fields have taken advantage of this opportunity. The reason is that we have become so conditioned to our second-class status as "popular authors", it is hard to even attempt to batter down the gates of literary prejudice. I noticed recently that of the hundreds of encomiums heaped upon Fulton Oursler when he died in 1952, not a single one mentioned that he was the famous mystery novelist, Anthony Abbot. His entry in most current encyclopedias still omit such facts. So this sort of holier-than-thou prejudice against the writers of both genre fiction and humor, is still, alas, very much with us.

Made in the USA
Lexington, KY
05 November 2010